C-SUITE CONFIDENTIAL:
CASE STORIES FOR THE HIGH-YIELD CONSULTANT AND THEIR CLIENTS

C-Suite Confidential:
Case Stories for The High-Yield Consultant and their Clients

Ira S. Miller

Table of Contents

Introduction, by Robert McIntyre, Chief Technology Officer, CISCO Systems

Management processes today are like the air we breathe, so ubiquitous and extensively published that we often take them for granted or don't even think about them ... or, how about: "another management 'how-to' book"? Or we deplore them if we are in a difficult management situation. Whether we are working for a Fortune 100 company or a start-up, we rely on proven management techniques to bring about whatever we need to happen in our daily lives. Furthermore, the increasing use of technology today makes us not only more productive but more independent and collaborative; making sound management not only necessary but requiring even more discipline as our work lives and personal lives start to merge. Soon we won't "go to work" but will decide to "do work" wherever we are and whenever we choose. Video conferencing (Telepresence, Face-Time, Skype), on-line meetings (WebEx, Go-To Meetings), and work-at-home rules will allow our work environment to reach deeply into the fabric of our lives.

That's what makes this book so relevant and so timely. A clear understanding of sound management technique is essential for those who will strive to survive in this new work environment. As Ira points out early in this volume, the growing gap between the academic description of management and the real world of "people management" in this new world is a key divide that needs bridging. And Ira is in a unique position to do this.

I've known Ira for over 30 years, and have always found him to be a fascinating and indeed remarkable man. His curiosity and intelligence, coupled with a career so deeply involved in management of difficult businesses, have given him the tremendous insight that he shares in this book. Ira has never been afraid to step outside the accepted norm, if he felt the need, for pursuit of a new area of excellence and understanding of people. This is what makes his knowledge and understanding so valuable and drives the core of this work. And his stories reflect that uniqueness. Another way to describe Ira's experiences: "It would be hard to make this stuff up"!

Looking forward, a clear understanding of real-world, proven approaches to solving difficult management issues will continue to improve the underlying management processes that make our businesses tick. The resultant capabilities of the next generation of management in this new, productive, collaborative atmosphere, even five years or a decade out, are virtually indescribable today!

That in the end is what makes this book so valuable – a thorough understanding of the past principles described herein will allow those that shape our management approach in the future to "get it right," enhancing our working lives in ways we cannot begin to imagine.

These stories need to be told, no matter where you are in your career.

From the Author

On the next few pages you will have "my story." I have had exceptional luck with mentors who have taken me under their wing (see the Acknowledgments section). They taught me the secrets of their leadership success.

This book is for experienced consultants who want to improve their connection with CEOs and senior executives. One of the most powerful tools for us consultants is stories. The right story at just the right time reveals more about the client's options, our own nature, and a bit of history; it is the way most adults learn.

The book is not meant to be read cover-to-cover, but rather to have individual stories plucked out for use in a specific situation. Therefore, each story is written as a stand-alone unit. To do this, I have repeated the necessary background material within each story.

These stories are meant to help the reader in three ways:

1. Trigger memories that lead to their own, unique stories

2. Use these stories, when appropriate, as educational material for their clients, and

3. Encourage them to listen for stories from others: clients, friends, business associates

Acknowledgments

After 40+ years in industry, there are way too many people I should thank for all they have done for me, my career, and my family. In recognition that we're in a world of lists, here's the top ten, or so.

My wife, Kathy: A beautiful person, fabulous mom, she moved our family with my career. She kept my ego in check when I needed it. It's been a life worth living because of her.

Mom and Dad (Vitee and Harold Miller): Besides all the nurturing and putting up with one angry teenager, they knew to send me for career counseling once I (unexpectedly) announced I wanted to go to college, rather than have a career as a musician.

Jack Kirker: Not the most demonstrative, Jack led by example. His standards were the highest I had ever seen. He raised the bar for all: subordinates, peers, and his managers. Jack fought for my promotion into my first leadership position. He then started to measure my performance against the next organizational layer, preparing me for my next assignment.

Rick Richardson: Entered my life as Jack's boss. We got along immediately. His standards were as high as Jack's. Rick, to this date, is the best operational general manager I have seen. He stretched me by assigning projects far outside my job scope. Rick shared his ideas, expanded my horizons.

Jim Norman: The best storyboard facilitator I know. Jim helped me, as a business leader, turn around organizations six times over 15 years. Each time we got better at it. Without his help, in each instance, we would have floundered for months before finding the right strategic path. Jim also made sure I was properly ushered into the world of consulting.

Our daughters, Alicia and Cyndi: Each has grown into a woman of substance. Alicia's talent for educating children for whom English is a second language is second to none. She is a constant reminder of what selfless dedication can accomplish. Cyndi's determination is a force of nature. She has found her professional calling as a physician's assistant. But to see her as the mother of twins … wow! I don't know anyone enjoying motherhood more than Cyndi.

Bob McIntyre: Bob and I were mentored by Jack and Rick at the same time. Our careers overlapped twice, and each time it was a joy to work with him. He's still in corporate America, busier than ever. Yet I know I can call him and he'll respond with insightful advice and counsel.

Bill Webb: Bill and I met late in my career and in a very difficult, politically charged environment. In many ways Bill is my third business mentor. He has helped me understand myself and provided important insights into the running of a business.

Carolina Chapter – Institute of Management Consultants: OK, it's not a person. Jim Norman introduced me to IMC before I left industry. He said I would find people there who are knowledgeable, capable, and caring. He was right. At the Carolina Chapter I have found friends – people who will share everything they know to help get me over a hurdle.

David Geier: At age 50 I took up golf. At 51 I met David, my first instructor. More than bringing down my golf scores (from 130s to the low 100s, now in the upper 80s), he linked the golf experience to life. I found out through David that my leadership style followed the teachings of Eastern religion. Also, we both love Maynard Ferguson and Buddy Rich.

To everyone else, and there are many, who furthered my education, protected me, looked out for my benefit… accept my heartfelt "thank you." Please let me know how I can return your kindness.

WHO AM I TO WRITE THIS BOOK?

The fact is I'm pretty average. I barely got out of high school. Graduated from Staten Island Community College. Flunked out of SUNY – Albany. Graduated from Pace University (College back then) with a degree in business administration.

The GE Experience

Financial Management Program

I joined the Financial Management Program at GE right out of college. The program is a combination of weekly classes and rotational assignments. The classes teach how GE evaluates its businesses. But to get a good grade, the student must not only study the material, he must truly understand it. The course work measures effort as much as knowledge. GE wants people who are not only smart, but will work hard as well.

The rotational assignments all come with the same goal: improve this job's contribution to the business. These are six- or 12-month assignments and you're the 15th person on the job; and you're supposed to improve it! There's a life lesson here.

Background Snapshot

Responsibilities
- President
- Chief Operating Officer
- Chief Financial Officer
- Senior VP-Marketing & Sales

Industry Experience
- 19 years at GE
  - CFO at two divisions
  - President at two divisions
- 5 years in Entrepreneurial Roles
  - Venture Capital backed
  - Leveraged financing
- 8 years at medium-sized firms

Industries
- Warehousing
- Transportation manufacturing
- Diagnostic imaging equipment
- Financial services
- Telecommunications
- Furniture rental

No one is hired to maintain the status quo or make things worse.

The ultimate goal for those of us in the Financial Management Program is to get a spot on the internal audit staff. After three to five years there, you could expect to become CFO of a GE business unit.

I finished in the top 10 percent of my FMP class and was offered a position on "Staff." My wife and I decided it was time to start a family and I certainly didn't want to be an absentee father, so I declined.

Transportation Group

That decision led me to Erie, PA, as a financial analyst for one of the GE manufacturing divisions. It was a turbulent time for the Transportation Group. There were four or five major, consolidating reorganizations over the next two years. The CFO of my original manufacturing unit, Jack Kirker, kept landing the CFO slot in each new consolidated business. Our final consolidated unit consisted of two P&L businesses and two manufacturing units.

We were leaderless for many months. Finally, the Group brought in Rick Richardson as Division President. At the same time, Jack fought to put me in the CFO role of the large Renewal Parts business. At 29 years old I was in my first executive position.

Rick asked me to be Acting President of the Renewal Parts business one year later. I did that until someone fully qualified was found. Rick had me run a few task forces to resolve critical problems, problems that were outside of finance.

During this assignment I was selected to attend the Managers Development Course at GE's Crotonville campus. One month in length, the program exposed us to some of the most intensive course work and innovative leadership concepts.

When Rick was promoted to run the Locomotive Division, he took Jack and me with him. There, in a much larger division than Renewal Parts, I had responsibility for supporting Sales, Marketing, and Engineering. My team was responsible for sales accounting, domestic and international credit and collections, financial analysis, and liaison with the Renewal Parts business. Rick had me doing international negotiations, contract and financing negotiations with Conrail, and developing special programs to deal with out-of-warranty equipment failures.

Medical Systems

GE's internal executive search process put me on a slate to run one of the businesses in Medical Systems. I was fortunate to win the assignment over a strong internal candidate. I'm now 35 and running a P&L center. I inherited a portfolio of excellent offerings, and the results were OK, but not where they needed to be. (No one is hired to maintain the status quo).

Through a great effort by my team, guided by some excellent market research, we increased profits five-fold over a five-year period.

Once more I was chosen to go to Crotonville, this time for the Business Managers Course. We were driven through the two-year Harvard Strategic Planning MBA program in one month's time. We would have five case studies to prepare each night. With the exception of the module on leadership integrity (which was taught by GE people), all the professors were from Harvard.

Computer Leasing

The next challenge was to integrate a new acquisition into GE Capital. The family moved to San Francisco. The business was leasing IBM computer systems to Fortune 50 companies (an extremely risky business since the initial cost of the equipment was not recovered during the initial lease term and technology changed very quickly). The acquired business had not booked any new volume in over three years. Our responsibility was to find a way to re-enter the market and book new business that would meet GE Capital's risk profile. With an unbelievable effort from a totally new staff, we figured out how to achieve our financial goals. In fact, we tripled our new business budget, with profitable business, in each of the first two years.

Beyond GE: The World of Venture Capital

Telecommunications

It was time to try something new. My associate from the Locomotive business, Bob McIntyre, had just accepted the presidency of a telecommunication start-up (LICOM). Almost his first words to me were: "Ira, I need someone to talk to. Someone who will understand the words I'm saying." I joined as CFO and became COO shortly thereafter. What a great experience! We were backed by eight venture capital firms. We had a great technology. Unfortunately, the market wasn't ready for it. Ultimately, the business was sold for the investors.

Furniture Rental

Our CPA firm at LICOM introduced me to CORT Furniture Rental. CORT was a division of Mohasco, a publicly traded company that was going private. CORT would be taken private in a separate transaction.

As CFO, there were three great challenges: (1) educate the management on the importance of cash flow, not just book profit; (2) establish a consolidation process that would result in accurate financial statements; and (3) harden the enterprise information technology system through a complete upgrade.

I learned a great deal about how to run a large, remote network of small businesses. We had 36 divisions rolling up into five regions. Each division was a complete business.

But, there are some places where one just doesn't fit in.

Back to Diagnostic Imaging

Captive Leasing

My job search uncovered that Picker International, a rival of GE Medical Systems, did not have a captive finance capability. I wrote the CEO, Cary Nolan, sharing my background and accomplishments at GE Medical Systems. It was a clumsy letter. But, as they say, timing is everything. Cary and his senior team had just decided they needed an equipment financing capability in order to compete in an increasingly financially strapped healthcare industry.

Along with Larry Miller (no relation; he's the good-looking one) and Al Velotta we established the Picker Financial Group (PFG). Within five years PFG was in the top 100 equipment leasing companies in the U.S.

Multi-Hospital Business Group

The health care market was changing rapidly. Hospitals were consolidating into Integrated Delivery Networks (IDNs). GE and Siemens had figured out how to market and sell to these new, large customers. Picker was only calling on individual hospitals.

Cary and the EVP-Global Sales and Service, Bill Webb, asked me to come up with a plan to attack this new customer segment. For the third time in my career I needed to fully staff a start-up or under-performing organization.

With the help of Greg Firestone and Tim Callahan, consultants at NCI, we figured out how this market worked. Mary Ann Waldron joined as the Director of Marketing. We developed new approaches to packaging products and services. Mary Ann's team developed 13 consulting capabilities to help an IDN better target their markets. We partnered with radiology influencers to get into hospital systems where Picker never sold before.

In the end, we increased sales by $97 million, contributing $27 million to operating profit.

Trex Medical

Bill Webb left Picker to be CEO at Trex Medical. The entire previous leadership team was gone. The Parent company, now Thermo-Fisher Scientific, wanted four of the five divisions combined and then grown.

I joined Bill three months later as SVP-Marketing and Sales. Once again it was time to reconstruct the organization. The four divisions had overlapping and competing products and distribution channels; and, of course, redundant management positions.

All of that was rationalized in the first six months. A new strategy was developed, and we started executing at the November 1999 Radiology Association of North America industry show (more than 14,000 attendees).

As it turned out, Thermo was going through its own upheaval. The board decided that the company's stock price was severely constrained because Thermo had expanded the number of businesses it was in – to the point that the Wall Street analysts couldn't understand the company. The decision: sell off 60 divisions in the next 12 months. Trex was number 60 on the list.

We learned about the decision in January 2000. Bill and I had the division sold in September.

Consulting and Giving Back

My wife (Kathy), her Mom, and I moved to Pinehurst ... to our "retirement" home. It's proven to be a great decision. Kathy's artwork has found exceptional acceptance. We've made good friends. I can play golf year-round.

Retirement, however, was out of the question.

I started Ira S. Miller, Inc. to help leaders reach their professional and personal goals. I've had the privilege of working on over 120 assignments at over 32 companies during the last 12 years.

With my sincere hope that this book will help you become The High-Yield Consultant you want to be, here are the case stories...

Best wishes,

BUSINESS STORIES

These stories are meant to provide The High Yield Consultant with 'borrowed" business experience: an experience they can share with a prospect or client, at the appropriate time, to help them gain insights in to their own, current situation.

While the stories are all true, they are my best recollection of the events. And, some details may be left out or simplified for the sake of brevity and clarity.

Businesses are Like Organisms

When I was at Pace University I took a class in management taught by Dean Mathews, Dean of the Business School. I will never forget the day he brought a visual aid to class: it was a fish in a jar. "What does this fish have in common with a business?" he asked. You can imagine the lively discussion as a bunch of 20-year-olds wrestled with trying to merge two separate universes, the world of finance and the world of water. The answer turned out to be ... survival. Maybe survival is the ultimate goal of a business, certainly a large, corporate enterprise. (Only six companies listed in the Dow Jones Industrial Average in 1970 were on the list in November 2009.)

Is this always the case? Recently I've seen a major consolidation in the area of medical equipment distribution. The individual companies, all family-based, were uniformly strong in their respective geographic markets. Why, then, were these companies sold to a large national chain, when the act of selling goes against the primary goal of survival? The answer lies in the fact that, for family businesses, there are drivers other than the business's survival. In the case of medical equipment distribution, the founders were approaching retirement age and their children had careers outside the family business. Selling the business funded the founder's retirement plans; and, in some cases, the family trusts. So my professor was right. The goal of any business is survival. But, the goal(s) of the business are secondary to the goals of the founder of a family-owned business.

My First Division Presidency

My first division presidency was at GE's Medical Systems Group (GEMS) running the captive leasing business. It was a very strange situation. All other financing of GE products was done by GE Capital. At GEMS, Tom Dollard and Norm Jensen had started this unit on the basis that the balance sheets of healthcare providers would not be understood by GE Capital. Therefore, GE Capital would not be able to be competitive (rates or terms) with other lessors specializing in the healthcare space; and that would not help GEMS sell more equipment. As strange as this may sound, they were correct at the time.[1] After nine years as Division President, Tom moved to another assignment within GE.

GEMS' leadership did not want a GE Capital person running this business. The internal head hunting function turned up my name since my organization at GE Locomotive was responsible for participating in the financing of the locomotives we sold (we were a guarantor in some cases). Norm and I vied for the job. I probably got the nod because they knew Norm's flat spots, but not mine.

Within the first week, my boss, Don White, called me into his office and delivered the following message:

"We have a nice little business here. It brings in $X.X million in profit. Don't do anything to screw it up."

Message received, I went back to learning the business and becoming a student of the industries (health care and financing).

Two weeks later I get a call from Don's boss, Walt Robb – well, his secretary. Walt wants to go to lunch.

Walt, Don, and I are at lunch and Walt observes that I've been on the job for three weeks now. "What are your plans?"

Remembering Don's instructions, I repeat that we have a nice profit center here and I'm going to move slowly with changes. Walt

---

[1] GE Capital is now providing all the financing for GEMS as well as other financing vehicles to the health care industry.

erupts. "I didn't hire you to keep the status quo. Figure out how you're going to improve your business and let me know what you plan to do!"

I learned two things that day:

1.   It's hard to swallow a hamburger after the boss jumps all over you, and

2.   We're NEVER hired to maintain the status quo.

Picker's CRM Implementation

Before CRM (Customer Resource Management) was a common phrase, Picker International decided knowledge about the customer needed to be shared. A common depository was envisioned, enabled by Lotus Notes' remote update capability.

There was a lot of whining and sniveling when the new system was rolled out (management had followed the traditional, top-down change-management process). The biggest complaints surrounded the time required by field personnel to update the database with new knowledge about the customer (changes in employees or job responsibilities, reporting on sales opportunities in other parts of the hospital system, trip reports, etc.) and the length of time needed for synchronization.

Once the new system was in place and training complete, a small, cross-functional group was assembled (about five people). These were full-time jobs; all were stationed at headquarters in Cleveland, OH.

The users of the new system were asked to contact this group if they encountered a problem with the system or had ideas on how to improve its functionality.

The group captured and categorized all the input. They made recommendations for making adjustments to an internal board of senior leaders.

Once it became obvious they were being listened to, the field started to take ownership of the new system – its integrity, usefulness, and improvement. By the end of the first year, the system was better than ever envisioned by management with only one complaint outstanding … doing trip reports.

CT 9800 Upgrade Program at GE Medical Systems

Background

In the early 1980s GE was a significant player in the diagnostic imaging market, but not the powerhouse the company is today. Cat Scanners (CTs) were in their formative stage. GE's product offering was the 8800. While GE had other products (Nuclear Cameras, X-ray, Ultrasound, etc), the next blockbuster product (MRI) was just entering the early development stage. CT was the product that needed to bring growth to GEMS.

New technology, which improved clinical evaluations, was the driving force behind increased sales. Although economic pressures that would eventually lead to Managed Care were emerging in the form of Diagnostic Related Groups (DRGs), they had not yet produced a major impact in capital equipment purchasing decisions.

GE Medical Systems (GEMS) had pioneered the financing of medical capital equipment by the manufacturer. This financing capability had been in place for ten years when GEMS introduced the 9800 CT.

A Brief Primer on Financing

There are two ways to finance the purchase of a capital asset: (1) a loan and (2) a lease. Under a loan, the buyer "owns" the equipment subject to fulfilling the terms of the loan agreement. A leased piece of equipment is "owned" by the financing institution (lessor). The user of the equipment (lessee) is paying to use the equipment during the lease term. Title to the equipment does not transfer as part of the initial lease term. There are tax consequences of ownership. In the early 1980s they were depreciation and investment tax credit. To a leasing company, these were legitimate vehicles to reduce the tax burden of their company.

A note to financial-savvy readers: For simplicity, variations on the above have been omitted. Adding technical complications does not enhance this story.

GEMS's Problem

The 9800 CT was a significant advance in clinical capability. The CT product management team took the 9800 CT to market in a traditional manner: buy the unit because of its clinical benefits. Concerns over the emerging economic pressures brought the hospital's CFO into the decision-making process. All of a sudden there were financial obstacles to buying the equipment demanded by the physicians. Hospitals that had bought a CT (GE or others) during the last one to four years still had significant, un-depreciated value on their books. Hospitals that had recently acquired a GE 8800 CT on a lease could not economically get out of the lease obligation; that included leases through GEMS' Financial Services Group. In short, economics was thwarting the effort to upgrade GE's installed base of 8800 to 9800 CTs.

Management's Approach

I wasn't part of the product division's discussions on how to overcome the new economic obstacles. But, we can imagine discussions on price, de-featuring, etc. All would cost significant margin. I do know I was asked what Financial Services could do to help out. I went to my staff, presented the problem to our experts. We couldn't figure out the alchemy required to retire a customer's asset, in the middle of its life, and not have a major hit on somebody's books (theirs or ours).

The Limitation of Mind Maps

GEMS's management (me included) was following our preconceived patterns for problem solving. Our 'Mind Maps' led us to conclusions that did not help this situation. We were limited by organizational alignment, internal measurement systems, and a confusing set of tax laws.

The Solution

Our sales manager, Dave Hintz, came to see me one day. "I want to run something by you. We might be able to help the 8800 situation." I remember not wanting to go through this one more time. My Mind Map said, "All the sales guys want is commissions. They don't care about my measurements." I knew that wasn't the case with Dave, but my Mind Map chimed right in. Luckily, I didn't follow my natural inclination.

Dave had done a lot of research. He learned exactly what components would be changed out to upgrade an 8800 to the 9800. The CT product division had given Dave a value they would place on the returned components (these components could be broken down for repair parts to support the 8800 installed base). The net result was that Financial Services would be given value for the returned components. This was a radically different approach than bringing back the whole 8800 CT and selling it in the used equipment market, which was the only alternative we had evaluated.

We ran the numbers. We could provide the financing structure to handle the upgrade program. It would result in somewhat lower returns than we wanted, but close enough to help out. (No one was changing the measurement system).

Dr. No Shows Up

My leading expert in financing raised the tax issue. By removing a substantial percentage of the installed 8800, we would be forfeiting the tax benefits taken by GE. That loss would kill the financial return to GE.

I asked for a full discussion with GE's corporate tax counsel. The conclusion? "We're not sure."

We agreed to take an aggressive stance and not recapture the depreciation. (It turned out not to be an issue at all. The computer leasing business had been dealing with upgrades in this manner for years. Our tax counsel and GEMS' Financial Services experts did not have exposure to that business or its practices.)

Critical Information is Known Outside the Executive Suite

There was a huge amount of management time spent to address this crucial issue of how to get 9800 CTs into the marketplace. It took one highly motivated individual to seek out the logical (but not usual) solution to the problem.

I don't remember the exact result of the 9800 upgrade program. What I do know is that GE became the world leader in CT market share as the 9800 installed base grew. The whole GEMS organization learned how to become more creative by working across the divisions for a common goal. A new trust was developed between the sales organization and Financial Services.

Launching Maxiservice®ii Financing at GE Medical Systems

The financing arm of GE Medical Systems (GEMS) had been in place for nine years when I joined as the Division President in 1980. Tom Dollard founded and ran the unit up until then. He and Norm Jensen (marketing) developed the concept of bundling equipment, financing, and equipment service into one monthly payment in the late '70s. They called it Maxiservice®.

A Revolutionary Idea That Didn't Catch On

The concept, while broadly available today, was revolutionary at the time. It provided the customer, the hospital's CFO, a vehicle to obtain the latest medical imaging technology along with the preventative maintenance and repair service it would need throughout the financing term, typically five years. The monthly payment was considered a rental for accounting purposes and therefore, was recorded as an expense rather than a liability by the hospital. This improved the hospital's balance sheet, providing the opportunity for additional bank borrowing to finance capital expansions. The payments were fixed, avoiding the (then) annual increase in service costs. The hospital could return the equipment at the end of the lease term with no further obligation. All in all, an outstanding offering for a technology-driven marketplace.

It was a great deal for GEMS as well. The service revenue was locked in since the lease could not be cancelled. Service contracts were typically ordered after the one-year warranty was about to expire. GEMS would be in competition with third-party service firms at that time. Getting the service commitment before the equipment was installed increased GEMS's market share for equipment service. GEMS also had a leg up at the end of the lease. We knew when to contact the hospital.

We could provide customized solutions at that time, including upgrading to another piece of GEMS technology. Any equipment returned at the end of the lease was known to be in excellent condition because it had received GEMS service for its entire life. That produced higher market value in the used equipment market.

So why was there virtually no Maxiservice® business in 1980?

A Misunderstood Market

GEMS's field organization divided the U.S. into four sections: Northeast, South, Central, and West. The common belief was that each section of the country had its own buying preferences. The Northeast was financially driven and purchased using Maxiservice®. The South and Central wanted to own the equipment. The West would do loans, but not lease. Maxiservice® was offered only under a lease at the time. The financing sales force, which supported the equipment sales organization, firmly believed in these regional stereotypes.

Getting the Facts

It had taken approximately two years for me to fully understand how the Financial Services business fit in to the broader business and political equation at GEMS. The business's supporters were executive management who enjoyed the incremental profits and understood the strategic importance of locking in the customer that was provided through financing. The detractors included the field sales and service organizations that saw financing as one more issue getting in the way of the equipment sale; the only thing they were measured on. The Financial Services business had reached a plateau of just under a $90-million portfolio because of the negative field attitude. My challenge was to figure out how to get the business growing.

I started with the customer. Why did one customer finance their equipment and another didn't? If they were going to finance, what would influence them to use the manufacturer rather than a third party, say their bank? We hired an outside market research firm to look into these and many other external and internal issues. There was a significant emphasis on the benefits of Maxiservice® and under what circumstances those benefits would be attractive to the customer.

The answers were extremely clear. We could identify which health care providers would be most likely to finance from a manufacturer and the type of financing they would require. We also found out that the benefits of Maxiservice® were universally valued by customers in all our markets.

Small Successes, But No Cigar

There is power in independently derived information!

First of all, I felt strongly that Maxiservice® would sell if it was just presented properly by the field sales force. That gave me the courage to implement incremental financial incentives for the Financial Services and equipment field sales organizations.

Secondly, the product marketing groups, heretofore neutral regarding financing, became more interested in packaging financing with their hardware offerings. The success of the CT9800 upgrade program didn't hurt! (See previous story)

But, despite all the facts about customer needs and additional incentives, the Maxiservice® product did not generate additional volumes.

Getting Rid of the Last Obstacle

Frustrated and tired at the end of yet another meeting to increase the acceptance of Maxiservice®, we were standing up to leave when Tom McDaniels, one of our financing sales people said: "Do you want to know why Maxiservice® isn't selling?" I couldn't believe my ears! "Tom, what do you know that you're not telling us?"

Tom pointed out that the real (remaining) problem was with the measurements on the Field Service organization. They were measured on the INCREASE in service revenue year over year. Maxiservice® level-loaded five years of service revenue. The effect was to have higher revenue in year one and two and lower-than-planned revenue in years four and five. Even though they had higher market share, it didn't matter if the measurement system was looking at revenue growth (and profitability, I might add).

It took only a matter of months to change the way service revenue was accounted for under a Maxiservice® lease. No revenue was awarded to service during the warranty period. After that, the contract service revenue was booked on a growing slope rather than level-loaded. There was no change in the total dollars booked. In fact, the profitability of the contract was not affected at all; all that changed was the timing of the revenue stream to the service division.

A Happy Ending

Within two years, Maxiservice® became the premier financing vehicle in the industry. Annual volume from that product alone quadrupled in those two years. The GEMS financing portfolio grew to $395 million by 1985, when I left GEMS to run GE Computer Leasing.

Epilogue

I returned to healthcare financing in 1992, joining Picker International to help start up its captive leasing business. At that time, neither Picker nor any other diagnostic imaging manufacturer had a Maxiservice®-like product in the market. They just could not figure out how to make it work.

GE Computer Leasing
(Decimus Corporation)

Background

A wholly owned subsidiary of Bank of America, Decimus Corporation financed large computer systems (mainframes and storage devices) usually through operating leases. The company was small by comparison to GE Capital, MetLife Leasing, and others that provided a broader range of financial services. However, the management at Decimus was competent, and they provided profits and a tax shelter for their parent company.

Bank of America's financial performance suffered in the early 1980s. They could no longer take advantage of the tax benefits derived from Decimus' leasing operation. Decimus was prohibited from doing business other than maintaining existing customer relationships. The company was put up for sale.

Computer leasing was considered very risky. Rapid changes in technology that were unforeseeable by the leasing community, the emergence of IBM Credit (a well financed captive of IBM and, believed by most, to have inside information regarding IBM's technology road map), and the nature of operating leases kept the large players in secondary positions in this area. Speed of decision-making was one of the keys to Decimus's success. Sufficient technological knowledge, although short of insider information, was also crucial.

Decimus's management continually held out GE Capital (the financial service industry's largest player) as the evil witch of the East (Decimus was located in San Francisco). They continuously identified the differences between the way Decimus and (their perception of how) GE Capital did business and treated their people.

Imagine the impact on the organization when it was announced in 1985 that GE Capital was buying Decimus Corporation! The fact was, there <u>was</u> a great deal of difference between the two companies;

not all "good" at Decimus and all "bad" at GE Capital. The cultures were certainly different, as were the methods for doing business.

Setting Strategy at GE Computer Leasing

The key to profitability in computer operating leases is the value of the used computer equipment at the end of the initial three-year lease term. This is called the Residual Value. GE Capital had one method for setting residual value regardless of the type of equipment; they hired outside appraisers to estimate future values every three to five years. That worked fine for trucks, telephone systems, printing presses, etc. Computer residual value estimates changed every quarter; sometimes significantly. It was clear the standard GE Capital approach would not work for computer leasing.

Neither would the old Decimus approach work within GE Capital. Decimus management had been highly autonomous under Bank of America. They made their decisions without oversight. Bank of America, interested in tax benefits and overall returns, left the day-to-day operations to Decimus management. GE Capital provided oversight for the assumptions (e.g.: residual value and return on investment targets) and let local management run the business. The problem at Decimus (GE Computer Leasing) was that there was no way to modify the assumptions or make timely decisions.

The leadership problem was how to bridge the gaps in culture, business processes, and decision-making speed between the computer-leasing environment and GE Capital's policies.

Culture

Ultimately the entire executive layer from the original Decimus left before the GE Capital acquisition or shortly thereafter. They saw no way of bridging the gaps and they wanted the autonomy provided by Bank of America. Most of the middle management and individual contributors stayed, providing a solid base for continuing operations.

Business Process and Speed of Decision-Making

GE Capital inserted its own president (me) and CFO (Ginny Horgan) into Decimus. The president had no prior computer leasing experience but had a very successful record in medical equipment leasing within

GE. Very swiftly the primary issue became how to write new business given the gap between industry practices and GE Capital's internal process.

The Enterprise Objective

This was easy: Become one of the largest computer leasing companies by leveraging GE Capital's strengths and bringing new products and services to market.

Developing Strategic Priorities and Action Plans to Achieve the Enterprise Objective

Learn How to do Business within the GE Capital Model

New business could be booked if each deal was run through GE Capital's exception process. This required a formal write-up for each transaction that included:

- Credit analysis

- Description of the equipment's technology and anticipated life

- Justification of the residual positions using independent industry data that was updated every three months

- Anticipated financial return

Develop a Team-playing Atmosphere

There were two elements to this. The first was within GE Computer Leasing and the second between GE Computer Leasing and the parent company, GE Capital.

Developing and sharing Mission and Vision statements went a long way to building the team approach within GE Computer Leasing. The very magnitude of getting the job done did the rest.

The linkage with GE Capital was never fully achieved. Geography played a significant role blocking the feeling of "team" from West to East coast. GE Capital's inability to adapt to the faster computer-leasing environment led, over time, to a feeling in San Francisco that "they just don't understand us."

To the credit of the initial management team, the business booked 300 percent of their budgeted volume in each of the first two years after the acquisition. The booked business proved profitable over time.

Choose the Technology in Which to Invest

An ex-Decimus executive was hired as an outside consultant to advise management on the state of technology and specifically which mainframe models were at the early stages of their technological life.

Set the Organizational Structure

Once the executive team understood that every transaction would require the extra effort associated with GE Capital's exception process, non-traditional positions were established.

The first was a Credit Analyst whose real job was to gather all the information about the transaction and generate a document that explained why GE Capital should approve the transaction. The individual was expected to apply their personal judgment before recommending approval. Many possibilities were never sent to corporate once the executive team understood the risk/reward scenario developed by the Credit Analyst. "This doesn't sound like a Credit Analyst's job!" you say? You're right. But, that was the closest "standard" position within GE Capital to what was needed. Using an existing title and position guide improved the timing of getting the position approved.

The second was a position that would sell off transactions that GE Capital would not approve. The GE Computer Leasing executives felt these transactions were sound, but without approval they could not be funded. This unique position found passive investors who would share the return on investment with GE Computer Leasing since they did not have the expertise to actively manage the assets. GE Computer Leasing retained the customer relationship and earned some income while avoiding any of the residual or credit risk.

Summary

This is an example of how the a creative leadership process was used to overcome market and internal culture issues.

Hiring the VP Layer at GE Computer Leasing

Two executive positions were filled when the new president of GE Computer Leasing (that would be me) arrived in San Francisco, the CFO (Ginny Horgan) and VP-Operations (Liz Hawk). The CFO came out of GE, while the VP-Operations was an internal promotion from within the old Decimus ranks. Both proved to be invaluable to the transition and early success at GE Computer Leasing.

Filling the Staffing Holes

The president applied the first law of organizational development: "Set the organization structure to fit the strategy." An idealized, unconstrained view of the future was developed in San Francisco and then presented to corporate management. The plan was accepted with the caveat that GE Computer Leasing lives within GE Capital's risk tolerance. The plan was in place with no executive team to execute it.

The challenge would be to hire six qualified executives into an uncertain situation and have them in place yesterday. I hired an executive search firm to handle all the positions simultaneously.

Lessons Learned from David Mather

David was working for Andersen Consulting and was assigned to the search. The first thing he did was understand our business situation. The disparity in culture between GE Capital and GE Computer Leasing necessitated hiring people who could deal with the inherent ambiguity. The next area was identifying the "flat spots" of the president and existing officers. These shortcomings needed to be shored up through the new hires. Finally, he identified what specific (technical & experiential) skills were required.

I like to think of this challenge as a simultaneous equation raised to the sixth power. Every individual on each candidate slate had to be considered in juxtaposition to every other candidate on the other slates.

The business was able to hire its complement of executive staff. All the up-front work forced on the president by David proved essential to reaching the company's goals. The team worked through the difficult issues identified in the previous case. They were able to establish routines that achieved almost all the goals established in the strategic plan.

But most importantly, they were able to make operating decisions as a team (reach consensus), freeing the president to work on the integration issues with GE Capital.

Moving from the Bell Operating Company to Industrial Market at LICOM

This is a story about business failure and personal growth.

First a disclaimer: my technical knowledge about telecommunications equipment would fit in a thimble. However, to tell this story I will have to use descriptions and terms that I understand and that may not be perfectly accurate. One thing is for sure; we had highly competent technical people at LICOM to help me with my understanding of the products.

The Opportunity to Leave GE

It's a long story as to why I left GE after 19 years of success, but this was a great opportunity.

Bob McIntyre went from GE's Locomotive Division to GTE's communications business in Phoenix. We worked closely together at the Locomotive Division. Bright and energetic, Bob quickly rose to the presidency of one of GTE's divisions. From there, a venture capital firm recruited him to take over the presidency of LICOM, a telecommunications start-up. This was the classic situation of replacing the founder with professional management as the company moved from its R&D to its marketing phase. Bob soon realized he needed additional, "professional" help. A mutual friend reunited us. Bob offered, and I accepted responsibility for the day-to-day operations at LICOM. The offer included stock options among other upside potential. Having the opportunity to grow a fledgling company provided the excitement.

LICOM's Promise

LICOM was founded with a product that acted as a huge circuit breaker on power lines. Basically, the equipment monitored the electric current going through the lines and would shut down the electric current at the next box if there were too much of a surge. LICOM had developed a very fast telecommunications device in order for the boxes to talk to each other. LICOM's founders saw an application for the telecommunications technology at switching stations run by the telephone company. That's right, THE telephone company: this was just before deregulation of AT&T. The founders had secured funding from a large venture capital firm. Seven additional VC firms had become investors over time.

By the time Bob and I joined LICOM, in 1987, the product had been developed and the initial marketing strategy was in place. The product was capable of sending messages at a rate 10 times faster than the then-current standard. It could handle voice and data on the same line. And, each box was programmable from a remote site. In theory, a Bell Operating Company (Baby Bell) could eliminate the need to send service personnel out to remote switchboxes to rewire the lines every time a phone number changed. This product could revolutionize telecommunications.

Sell to the Bells

We inherited the strategy of getting the new technology in to the Baby Bells. The sales force was rich in selling experience to AT&T. They understood the technology. They understood the process. Bell South was targeted for beta testing. Once complete, Bell South would re-do its system, placing orders that would cumulatively reach $100 million. Other Baby Bells would follow.

Anticipating Success

In retrospect, we committed the greatest error one can make in a start-up situation: we staffed for success.

Some things had to be done. Manufacturing had to be put in place. Marketing programs needed to be developed. There was never any doubt that if we built it, they would come. We failed to apply the risk tolerance formula:

- What's the probability of failure?

- What's the penalty for failure?

No one thought the probability of failure was high. We should have all seen that the penalty for failure was disaster.

Understanding Your Customer's Situation Is Crucial

Six months went by. A dozen commitment dates from Bell South went by. There were no sales in sight!

What was going on? What had changed from the time the founders set forth on this strategy?

The market had changed dramatically. AT&T had been split into eight Baby Bells. Each Baby Bell was now in a competitive (rather than monopolistic) environment. The palette of opportunities for them was endless.

One can only imagine what was going on inside Bell South at the time. Management focus had to be on their Enterprise Objective. Internal processes and decision-making was in flux, as was the personnel making decisions.

The LICOM market strategy emulated the selling activity that was successful with AT&T. We were presenting a new technology when the old technology was adequate. We were asking people to make career-limiting decisions when those people were unsure of where they stood in the new organization. We were selling technology to the operational layer when the real decision needed to come from top management – and they were occupied with survival in a suddenly competitive universe.

Changing the Game Plan

This quarter's Board presentation was going to be in conjunction with LICOM's first industry exhibit in Atlanta. Bob and I were staying at the Omni hotel where CNN broadcasts originated. We were reviewing the overheads one last time (this was before PowerPoint let you change slides on the fly). I was good at communicating a story, but Bob was (is) a master. We were on his inside balcony overlooking the CNN studios, iced tea and mixed nuts at the ready. Bob was talking through the story.

The story was the same as last quarter. No orders yet from the "Bells," but they are still interested. Personnel changes are delaying decisions. We have a new set of target dates for key events. Meanwhile we're burning cash.

About half way through I interrupted Bob and said: "Do you believe any of this?" Bob and I always had a strong and open relationship. Very similar value systems, the GE upbringing, and having the same mentors (Rick Richardson and Jack Kirker) allowed us to communicate very quickly and succinctly. It was one of the reasons I enjoyed working with him.

We had done things right. That is, the management processes were in place and working. Now it was time to face the leadership question: "Are we doing the right thing?"

Bob stopped and thought. "What other plan could we put in place? What have we learned so far from our selling efforts?" Some of our sales people, faced with no success at the Baby Bells, had explored sales into industry. The inherent security of the box and the speed of transmission made it a great candidate for government agencies and defense contactors.

Bob took out the grease pens he always carried. He redid the overheads using the failed activities as a jumping off point to suggest a new plan was required.

The presentation went well and the board gave its consent for Bob to bring forth a new strategy.

Too Little, Too Late

Going to the industrial market made progress almost immediately. The new product line went from virtually zero to $4.0 million is sales. But this was a far cry from the hoped-for $100+ million in the minds of the investors.

The lead investor ultimately decided to sell LICOM. I later found out some of the investors wanted to continue with the new strategy, but that road was not taken.

What is Failure Anyway?

My adventure at LICOM lasted around 18 months. We didn't cash in on the options. Nor did we see the company grow as we had hoped. Yet, I can't find another year and a half where I learned as much.

- The risk formula works, one just has to remember to use it.

- Doing what's right has rewards of its own.

- I learned how the departments in a manufacturing business interrelate.

- I was able to implement the processes I was taught at GE and found they worked (in a simplified form) in small businesses as well.

- Exposure to the venture capital world taught me how businesses are capitalized, their stages of development, and the unique requirements at each stage.

I participated in a "failure" for the first time, and survived. The next test would be my recovery time. When could I get focused on moving forward? It didn't take long.

Designing a New Enterprise Computer System at CORT Furniture Rental

The Tax Partner at LICOM's auditing firm recommended that I speak with CORT Furniture Rental's CEO, Bob O'Malley. CORT had been a division of MOHASCO that was being taken private by a venture capital firm through a leveraged buyout. The division had been successful within the MOHASCO family, but it now needed to stand on its own; especially in the area of cash management. My GE financial background and general business understanding must have convinced Bob to bring me on board. The financial system for the company had to be, and were, totally revamped. But there was a much bigger problem; the computer system was made up of individual PCs, one per district.

Identifying the GAP

Trying to close the books each month was a major chore. Each district (36 of them) would close and send the information to their Region (5 of those) that would re-key in the data and close and send the information to corporate where the data would be re-keyed in order to close the company's books. The numbers wouldn't add up. Errors occurred at each transfer of data. Frankly, this was not a big problem when CORT was a $100 million division out of MOHASCO's $600 million. As a stand-alone entity, however, it needed its books to be accurate.

The accuracy of the books and the pain and suffering to generate the closing was only one of the symptoms of the real disease ... the lack of information to run the business. Another symptom was the write-off every year of $1 million in physical inventory deficit. We could never be sure if it was caused by theft, poor procedures, or erratic bookkeeping. Finally, each region was defining the table of accounts differently. Therefore, when we added up the individual revenue lines, we were adding apples to oranges to pears.

The GAP was the lack of data integration.

Bringing in the Experts

We hired Andersen Consulting (currently Accenture) to help us design and implement (see the next case study) an integrated, enterprise-wide information system. The problem was that each district (that's right, district) had its own way of handling each of their business activities. All the business systems were manual. Therefore, each district could design their own forms, process paper at different times during the cycle, and overcome customer issues with infinite flexibility. Accountability and understanding business performance were sacrificed. How does a company with a culture of decentralization to the nth degree decide on the requirements of an enterprise-wide system?

A Major Test for Storyboarding and Jim Norman

With the concurrence of Bob O'Malley, the region VPs, and executive staff, my director of IT and I hired Jim Norman to run consecutive storyboard sessions to extract the critical data elements needed to run the business. Unfortunately, storyboard sessions are limited to 20-25 people in order to be successful. At the same time, we needed to get the information pulled together in such a way that it made a coherent, integrated story.

We decided to bring in one or two functions (departments) at a time for an intense one or two day session. The region VPs assigned the appropriate people from their territories. Bob helped ensure that the most knowledgeable employees as well as the "Dr. Nos" were included. My memory says we went 10 days without a stop. The schedule was something like this:

- Dinner for the arriving group(s), let's say marketing and sales. This included an introduction to the Andersen people and the new corporate IT team.

- Introduction to the system project

- Introduction to storyboarding

- Running the storyboarding session. Identifying all the data elements for their function. Grouping them together logically. Comparing their needs to the available software functionality. Compromising where required. Recycling as new items were thought of.

- Thanking the group and presenting mementos of the activity.

- Then dinner that night with the next group.

Without storyboarding techniques, we would have never been able to capture the vast amount of information required to define the system.

Defining the System

The cumulative outline of all the storyboard sessions ran over 100 pages. Amazingly, the folks at Andersen were able to develop a proposal around the requirements extracted from the teams. The proposed system would handle all the standard business functions (accounting, customer masters, inventory, etc.). Even after extensive programming, the many unique manual processes would have to be subjugated to a single computer-acceptable process. This would be the most expensive single project ever undertaken at CORT.

Moving Forward

The troops were energized! Everyone, it seemed, believed CORT needed a centralized system that would provide additional information to run the business. The next step was to select experts from each of the functions to create a core team that would interface between the Andersen people and the CORT people. The selection wasn't easy, but they were chosen and moved to CORT's headquarters in Fairfax, Virginia.

The next six months would really be exciting.

Implementing the Enterprise Computer System at CORT Furniture Rental

Looking back, Andersen Consulting, the IT team, and the Raleigh beta site group all did an excellent job of getting the new system ready for roll out. Why, then was the system killed?

Dealing with Tasks and Avoiding Culture

Building the System

A detailed game plan was put together and approved by Bob O'Malley and the CORT executive team. Implementation was fairly typical, I'm told. Unforeseen linkages and processes required additional programming. Managing a young and fluid programming staff at Andersen added to the challenge and probably caused some delays. But overall the system was developing by piecing together hardened modules from Andersen, an accounting software package, and the custom software; all running on IBM hardware. The full package came in a few months late and close to budget.

Management's "Oh, my God"!

You may recall from the previous story that CORT was highly decentralized. Thirty-six districts were each running independently of each other. Accounting was consistently maintained within each of the five regions, but not necessarily consistent across regions. In addition, any explanation of variance from plan was only available from region management. Substantive activities could go unnoticed unless one was willing to perform a massive operational audit and review every transaction every month.

The new system was going to end all of this by standardizing on an account structure and allowing the corporate controller to drill down through any journal entry to the originating documents. In addition, operational procedures would be standardized in each district so that cash, inventory, and other asset controls uniformly met standard controllership guidelines.

For some reason, operating management did not fully understand how the system would impact their daily lives until the beta test was started. This was after six months of what I thought was over-communication regarding the system and how it would change the business. I think the final *"Oh, my God"* came when the system revealed that the inventory controls at the beta test site were unacceptable in many ways. This site was considered one of the best sites for inventory control before the system's installation.

Addressing Culture

I don't know for sure if even a massive attempt to address the culture issues would have allowed the system to survive. I believe, in this case, the management culture of virtually complete independence from corporate oversight would have killed any attempt to implement a centralized system.

Lesson(s) Learned

The depth of the corporate culture cannot be overestimated! Mere facts, even the company's survival, may be subordinated to the culture. Peter Bregman, an absolute guru regarding implementing change, says there are three attributes of change:

1. Ownership
2. Capability, and
3. Persistence

In the CORT situation, operating management did not have ownership, and the corporate leadership did not have persistence. While the system itself was successfully developed and ready for implementation, the project was doomed from the first.

Establishing Market Pricing at Picker Financial Group

Picker International manufactured and serviced diagnostic imaging equipment sold to healthcare providers. For years they were losing business to GE Medical Systems (GEMS) due to GEMS's ability to package equipment, service, and financing (Maxiservice®, see earlier story). In 1991 Picker made the decision to set up its own finance company. This is the story of one of many start-up problems that threatened to kill the new entity, Picker Financial Group (PFG).

Applying the Risk Rules

Picker's management understood that both the probability of failure and the penalty for failure were significant in this new venture. After all, the landscape was littered with failed healthcare financing companies. Mitigating this risk was crucial to their plan. The solution: bring in a knowledgeable partner.

The Problem with Partnerships

A joint venture was formed with a local leasing company that had extensive experience in computer leasing, but none in medical equipment. From the beginning, each partner tried to force incremental risk on the other. This new venture was not the core business of either partner, but could be the death of their respective enterprises if things got out of hand.

The net result was a business that just would not function in its market. A few of the problems were:

- A capitalization structure that exaggerated the cost of capital

- Credit limits (authority) within PFG were so low that virtually all business had to be reviewed by the board

- Credit write-ups were so cumbersome that PFG could not respond with reasonable speed in the marketplace

- ROI targets were set at the highest level ever achieved within the leasing company partner's history – far above market norms

- Residual value assumptions were calculated at one-half the expected value

You get the idea. Each partner eliminated its potential risk through policies and guidelines that precluded any chance of being competitive in an established market.

When Failure Occurs

A financing sales force had been hired. They were compensated through a base salary and commissions for new business. When the first pricing matrix came out, which accommodated all the above risk avoiders, the sales organization knew immediately they were out of business. To make matters worse, Picker Financial Group was introduced to the entire domestic sales force with great fanfare at the annual send-off. Talk about falling on your face coming out of the blocks.

This may not look like it, but this situation requires many of the same steps as any leadership challenge.

- Know where we are

- Envision where we want to be

- Design a game plan to bridge the GAP

- Develop the action plans to build the bridge

Gathering Data

I believed any change in pricing assumptions would have to be fact-based. The only way to get enough information was to work hard at getting business even though we knew we would lose almost all the deals.

The second piece of information required was the details of the winning transaction. This was very hard to get. We solicited the help of Picker's sales force. They were able to get the information from the customer in an overwhelming number of the transactions.

The PFG sales team did this for nine months! Morale was a disaster within PFG and the broader Picker sales organization.

Creating Information

I was able to reverse-engineer each lost transaction in which GEMS was the winner. A consistent story emerged that mirrored the packaging that was developed between 1980 and 1985 at GEMS when I was running the Financial Services business.

Disseminating Knowledge

As a new entity, and a new joint venture, PFG had monthly board meetings. The president and CFO of each partner company were on the board.

Each meeting included a presentation of won and lost business. Initially we could only identify the losses and show our offering. A much more detailed analysis was presented once the competitive information was obtained and we could identify the implied pricing strategy being used by GEMS. We recommended market-based pricing at each meeting, along with suggestions for sharing risk.

I was very, very impatient throughout this process. I now realize what we were really accomplishing was the education of the board members. The education was both about how the market worked and how they would have to align themselves regarding risk.

By the end of the eighth board meeting, it was clear both sides understood the situation, knew what needed to be done, and were, apparently, not willing to change the business model.

Life Is Too Short

Earlier I mention that Bob McIntyre and I had developed a shorthand way of communicating. "Life is too short," between us, meant that the pain and suffering of doing what's right was affecting the important things in life such as health and family relations.

So it was at Picker Financial Group. Not just for me, but also for the sales management who had to try to explain PFG's apparent disregard for market conditions to prospects and the equipment sales force. No one was happy. No one wanted to come to work in the morning.

This was the attitude going into the ninth board meeting.

Sometimes the Facts Don't Matter

The same bleak story and the same analysis and the same recommendations were presented. The difference was that all the PEG officers made it clear we were tired of the situation. We didn't threaten to leave or do anything rash. We merely pointed out that we did not believe we could deliver acceptable business results given the board's position on pricing and risk-tolerance.

I can only imagine the change the board saw. This was an energetic, smart, and creative group of leaders coming into a board meeting with their tails between their legs. I firmly believe the board members reacted as much to management's emotional state as they did to the fact that we weren't making any headway for the business.

All's Well That Ends Well

The pricing structure changed within 15 days. Over time, the partners learned how to negotiate to acceptable risk positions. Within four years Picker Financial Group's portfolio size ranked it in the top 100 leasing companies in the United States.

A Selected Postscript

What happened to the sales people for whom a large percentage of their compensation was tied to booking business?

Three calendar quarters had passed and there was no way to get back to budget. Management presented an equitable way to reward those sales people who were working hard for PFG. The board, to their credit, accepted the proposal that kept our best sales people at their targeted compensations level.

I learned an important lesson from Cary Nolan, President and CEO of Picker, in that session. He made it clear that it wasn't meeting the numbers that mattered, but rather, retaining those sales professionals that who would take the company to the next level.

Developing the Strategic Plan at Multi-Hospital Systems Business Group

What a mouthful: Multi-Hospital Systems Business Group! Think "National Accounts" with attitude.

Picker International manufactured, serviced, and financed diagnostic medical equipment; CAT scanners, MRIs, x-ray, and nuclear cameras. They competed with some small companies like GE, Siemens, Philips, Toshiba, etc. Picker was having significant growth (sales and income) under the leadership of Cary Nolan (CEO) and Bill Webb (EVP-Global Sales & Service). One area that was underachieving was National Accounts. There was the usual rift between field sales and national accounts as to who should get credit for a given sale. The measurement systems could not identify any incremental value to the national accounts program. And Picker's leadership for the product businesses (P&L centers) placed little value on national account activity, which they perceived as doing nothing but attempting to lower margins. This state of affairs existed for ten years while the traditional methods of doing business were finding exceptional success for the company.

During 1996, Cary and Bill decided to "fix" the National Accounts area. Through interviews with industry candidates they discovered that the competition had embraced a national accounts strategy and was starting to experience positive results. Picker management didn't know how to get started or what it would take to be successful.

In the fall of 1996 I was asked to leave Picker Financial Group and take over Picker's national accounts activity. I accepted, with some trepidation, due to Cary and Bill's assurance that they would provide whatever I needed to be successful. That is a good question. What will the National Accounts Group need to be successful?

Determining the Current Situation

National Accounts had been tucked under Government Accounts. Doug Larm ran the unit ably. However, he was not able to convince Picker management of the need for a strong National Accounts organization. I started with Doug, and over four or five sessions he provided me with an excellent understanding of National Accounts history within Picker and his impression of the various customers and players in the industry. I interviewed each of the four National Account reps next.

My initial conclusions:

- There was no definition of a "national account"

- The product managers were solely in charge of developing the approach for all national account programs

- Doug could not identify his successes since all the bookings were only identified with their associated field sales office

- Two of the four reps had retired on the job

Where Do We Need To Be

Some input was received through structured interviews with Doug and the reps, but this certainly wasn't the view of the whole organization. I set up 15 one-hour interviews (all covering the same open-ended questions) with each of the product line general managers, field sales management, field sales personnel, and field service management. The results were startling, especially regarding what National Accounts should be.

Some the responses were:

- Identify opportunities for multiple purchases and turn them over to the field sales office

- Develop unique programs for large purchasers independent of the product managers

- Direct the sales effort of any transaction where the customer is buying two or more units

- Provide advice in the design of new products that represent the needs of large customers

Two things were clear to me:

1.   There was no consensus as to the proper role for National Accounts, and

2.   All the suggestions were tactical.

We needed a strategy that would be bought by the whole organization

Setting the Strategy

This was yet another job for Storyboarding to identify the GAPs and get to THE answer quickly.

NOTE: Rick Richardson, one of my mentors, used to say: "Don't bring me AN answer (to the problem). I want THE answer." Clearly some problems have more than one answer. Rick was challenging us to see beyond the obvious and get to the best answer.

Step One – Selling the Need for a Strategy

Picker's executive staff was stuck in business as usual regarding National Accounts. In a half-hour presentation at the weekly staff meeting I presented the input from the interviews and a preliminary view of the national account market. I was able to identify three separate markets. Each required a different, specific approach, but a similar process could serve all the segments. I stopped there, even though I had a good idea of what I wanted to recommend. What I did recommend was that a team come together for a one-day session to develop the strategy that would guide Picker's National Account effort.

Step Two – Selecting the Players

There are a few rules for this step:

1.   The total cannot exceed 20-25 people for the storyboard session.

2.   Ensure the Dr. Nos are included. These are the people who have a vested interest in the status quo or are just against change in general.

3.   Have every affected organization represented.

4.   Include as many "informal" leaders (influencers) as possible.

This takes a lot of effort. There will be tradeoffs. Strive for THE answer.

But at Picker we had another problem. There were warring factions on the executive staff. Any consensus developed by the Strategy Team would quickly be killed by one of the two factions, one of which was my boss, Bill Webb. Using the same logic as in rule #2 above, I established a three-member Board of Directors for the project (remember, I had the complete support of Picker's President and CEO, Cary Nolan). They were Bill Webb, Tim Hansen (the most influential of the product general managers, and the other warring chieftain), and Jerry Cirino (well respected general manager of a supplies distribution business which had its own National Accounts organization). The executives consented to be briefed on the process before the meeting and to hear the results of the Storyboard session, but not to participate in the Storyboard session itself.

Step Three – Setting the Stage and Developing the Strategy

Once the dates were set, I called Jim Norman, storyboard guru. Jim and I met by phone so I could explain the situation to him. We went through the business issues, internal politics, competition, and my expectations for this meeting.

The entire process was scheduled to take one full week:

Monday:	Display the process to the Board. Obtain their input on any missing elements or issues.
Tuesday:	Preview the Storyboard session with Jim. Jim performs a Structured Interview on me and selected staff members to get the latest information. We then envision the entire Storyboard session in an attempt to identify the contentious issues and where the Dr. Nos will

insert negativity. We developed a strategy to deal with the envisioned problems. Jim uses the evening to develop "headers" that will speed up the Storyboard session process without leading the team to any specific conclusion.

Wednesday: Jim facilitates the Storyboard session. The team identifies what role National Accounts needs to fill in the marketplace for Picker. They write the Mission Statement. A high-level Action Plan is developed.

Thursday: Jim, the selected staff members and I debrief the Storyboard session. We summarize the information and thoughts. We develop the presentation to the Board.

Friday: The results of the Storyboard session are presented to the Board. They ask a lot of questions, most of which have been answered in the Storyboard session. They provide additional insights. They agree with the Strategy.

This is an exhausting process. The dividends of the process, not the specifics of the strategy, are paid over and over again when the warring factions take aim at National Accounts (now Multi-Hospital Systems Business Group [MHS]) and my defense is: "You agreed to the strategy. We're executing. It is successful. Why do you want to change now?"

Step Four – Communication

The attendees of the Storyboard session team did an excellent job of disseminating the results of the session. In addition, everyone in MHS made presentations to the product management groups and field offices to share the strategy. MHS personnel attended the product group and field sales staff meetings, usually with time on the agenda for MHS updates and success stories. All this AFTER I presented the MHS strategy to field management at Picker's national sales meeting that kicks off the fiscal year.

The Results

The Strategy, based on an understanding of the markets serviced best through a centralized sales and marketing organization, kept us focused. The MHS marketing team led by Mary Ann Waldron, developed consulting-type products that were made available to all the sales force to address the needs of large purchasers of Picker's products. Special programs were developed between MHS and each of the product management groups to win large, committed contracts. In the end, MHS could demonstrate incremental sales around $100 million per year with no material reduction in profitability.

Reorganizing Marketing and Sales at Trex Medical

This is a horror story! The company was plagued with problems; a parent company that was seeking a clear vision for itself, five divisions within Trex that ran autonomously with little oversight, some of the Trex divisions competed with each other through competing dealer networks, and the implied strategy of growth through acquisition was failing. The net result was predictable: plummeting financial results. New corporate management was hired to consolidate the four medical divisions and grow the business.

The Inherited Situation

The new CEO had made the decision to consolidate the manufacturing facilities as a way to improve efficiency. Five production facilities would become two. However, what to do about the product lines was left to the newly appointed SVP-Marketing and Sales (yours truly).

The Current Situation

Interviews were immediately held with all the marketing and sales executives of each of the divisions. Amazingly, there was complete unanimity that the company needed to be consolidated. It was clear that each division had its own view as to how the new organization would be organized.

If a consolidation of the marketing and sales functions were to take place, there would be a need for a marketing and sales staff at Trex's corporate layer (as opposed to each division). There was no time to do searches. The new positions would have to be filled by the existing staff, no matter how qualified.

There was also an urgent requirement for the new SVP to get a first-hand view of the capabilities of the individual divisions. Business reviews focusing on marketing were held at each facility.

My impressions of the individual divisions' approaches to their business, marketing and sales personnel, and a recommended going-forward strategy were presented to the Trex executive staff. The approach was blessed, resulting in the naming of the corporate marketing and sales staff. However, no decision regarding consolidation or the specifics of product line rationalization was made at that time.

Modified Specifics, the Same Process

I had to develop my personal GAP Analysis in a very short period of time. I joined Trex Medical in mid-March. The new staff was named before the end of June. All marketing and sales personnel were informed of their new responsibilities by the end of July.

Before announcing the new corporate marketing and sales staff, an expanded group of marketing and sales personnel were brought together for a three-day meeting to discuss (and hopefully agree on) how marketing and sales should be organized. A modified version of the storyboard GAP analysis was used. The group identified the current situation along with their collective vision for what Trex would have to become to generate improved financial results. The meeting started with personnel from each division sitting together, shoulder to shoulder. There was open dislike for personnel in divisions with competing products. I was pleased and astonished to observe the transformation. The discussions revealed the depth of market knowledge in the room. The unanimity for consolidation surprised many in attendance. The group easily agreed to the identification of Trex's strategic advantages and the vision for Trex's future. While the overall direction towards consolidation did not change as a result of the retreat, certain specifics regarding organization structure and people to fill key positions were different than my pre-retreat thinking.

The Unknown Factor

Rationalizing the overlapping product lines and distribution channels did not go smoothly, but it got done. Old loyalties arose. Personal goals became disconnected from the functional goals that were supporting the corporate strategy. Executive management failed to continuously communicate the corporate goals or express a vision that went beyond improving the bottom line.

Despite all the obstacles, a cogent strategy was implemented. Financial results improved (as measured by orders and sales) in December and January.

On January 29th the parent company announced that it would sell 60 divisions representing more than 30 percent of its revenue. The objective was to clearly focus on their core business, thereby providing a clear vision for the company's future to Wall Street analysts. The stock went up, validating the strategy.

Meanwhile, back at Trex the news that Trex would be sold came as a massive body blow. The parent company had added Trex to the "for sale" list at the last minute. Therefore, there were no potential buyers identified. The market for Trex products collapsed, given the uncertainty surrounding the company. The best distributors (mostly closely held organizations) immediately started talking to competitors. Trex personnel, after working through the most difficult business issues they had ever encountered, were devastated.

Trex was sold eight months later.

A Final Thought

Leadership occurs most visibly during a crisis. Leaders are tested during a crisis. But, for most of us, the test of our leadership capability occurs daily, in small ways. Being consistently effective as a leader prepares us for crisis (should it arise), but also allows us to raise our organizations and its people (and ourselves) to the next level.

LIFE LESSONS

It's been my experience that many, many people have had serious, and sometimes profound, effects on me and my life. As you will see below, not all are from the business world.

The stories chosen all have, I believe, a lesson for business leaders. These can be shared by The High Yield Consultant with prospects and clients to help with a specific issue or hurdle that they are facing.

Again, these are true events and related here through my best efforts, if somewhat foggy memory.

First, Do What's Difficult

1958

"Dad, I want to play drums." My parents were thrilled about my music ambitions. But they had one requirement: "You must take lessons."

My first lesson with Tommy (I don't remember his last name) was how to hold the sticks and feel the bounce when striking the pad (low-noise substitute for a real drum) and showing me how to play the first page of exercises in the *Stick Control* book.

For the second lesson, I had to play the practiced lessons for Tommy. After I did, he pointed to two of the exercises and said: "You don't like to play these. They were harder for you." I admitted he was right. His next statement has stayed with me to this day; talk about a life lesson:

"Ira, you need to work harder on the exercises you don't like. They're the ones that are more difficult for you and will take longer to master."

In my business life this has meant looking at the tasks in front of me (as a leader, manager, or individual contributor) and choosing to work on the ones that I don't like first. Work on them when I'm fresh, clear-minded, and least stressed.

Take Away

Organize the workload so that the unpleasant tasks are handled before the ones you like to do.

Key Words

- *Organizing*
- *Prioritize*
- *Prioritization*

Completed Staff Work

1978

Bob McIntyre and I were asked by Rick Richardson (Division President, GE Locomotive) to make a recommendation to the division staff; I don't remember the specific topic or issue.

It was not unusual for meetings to start well after 5 PM, and so it was with this one. I was presenting the overhead slides (yes, way before PowerPoint). This slide had the recommendation, but Bob and I had not fully agreed on the approach. The slide showed two recommendations.

Rick stopped the meeting. It was probably around 7 PM. He said something like: "You are asking me to make the decision. I'm probably the least qualified of anyone in this room to make this decision. You and Bob work it out and we'll reconvene at 7 AM."

Bob and I worked late into the night and presented our one recommendation the next morning to the full division staff.

Take Away

Leaders need to set the expectation of completed staff work. It expands the capabilities of the staff and reinforces accountability.

In this one action, Rick made his expectations clear to Bob, me and his entire, assembled staff.

Key Words

- *Completed staff work*
- *Accountability*
- *Delegation*

Becoming the Market Leader

1977

The Generals, General Motors and General Electric, pretty much divided up the global locomotive market, 76% GM and 24% GE.

The price of fuel was skyrocketing for the railroads. We were in this year's first strategic planning meeting where a picture of the environment (customer's industry, government regulation, global economic and political forces, etc.) were laid out by our internal strategic planning department.

The issue of fuel cost was brought up by our VP-Marketing and Sales, Jack Dwyer. He was hearing this concern from the presidents of all the railroads (12 back then). The strategic planners pointed out that fuel was only 5 percent of the railroads' total cost, and therefore should not be a major economic issue.

Dwyer and Rick Richardson (Division President) were of the opinion that if it mattered to the railroad presidents, it should matter to us. What could we do to reduce their fuel costs? The discussion continued for awhile.

Then, out of nowhere, our VP-Engineering (think R&D) said: "There's a lot of technology available that if applied to a new series of locomotives would improve fuel costs, reduce maintenance, and be less expensive to manufacture." He used recent product changes in the automobile industry as examples of how that technology was being applied.

The New Series locomotive became part of our strategic plan. The first units were delivered in 1980. While I left the Locomotive Division in 1980, I stayed in touch. Within two years the market shares had reversed (GE 85%, GM 15%). Then, in the recession that followed, GE went to 100%.

Take Away

Listen to the customer. As a supplier, our logic may not be what's driving the customer's decisions. Marketing/Sales needs to be the voice of the customer inside any business.

Great, game-changing ideas come from many places in the organization. Leaders need to establish an environment of purposeful creativity where all ideas are truly heard and considered.

Key Words

- *Creativity*
- *Strategy*
- *Strategic planning*
- *Customer*

Courage to Become the Market Leader

1978

I was sitting in Rick Richardson's office (Division President, GE's Locomotive Division) going over my slides (overheads) for the quarterly business review when the phone rang. Rick said he had to take the call. I asked if I should give him some privacy. He said: "No."

All I remember is that it was a contentious conversation about the New Series locomotive that was in development. Rick said "OK" at the end of the call.

After he hung up, Rick told me the call came from an individual who was a few layers higher in the GE hierarchy telling him to cancel the project. Then he called the VP-Engineering to make sure the project was on schedule.

He looked back at me, pointed out that he did not respect this individual (maybe he said it more strongly), and told me that this was the most important decision he was going to make as President of the Locomotive Division and he will see it through.

Take Away

Courage is when you put your beliefs ahead of politics.

Key Words

- *Courage*

Career Choice

1980

Since I started at GE my goal was to be CFO of a business unit. I achieved that goal at age 29. I was now in my second, similar assignment and ready to move on.

At the time, the finance function within GE had an individual (Chuck Steers) tasked with putting the appropriate people on slates for executive finance positions. Chuck had me on a slate for the Group CFO slot at a Virginia business group (multiple divisions report in to a group). The interview went well, I thought.

A few days later Rick Richardson (Division President for the business I was in) calls me up to his office. He tells me he just got off the phone with the hiring manager (Group Executive) talking about me. Rick gave me a strong recommendation.

Then he asked if this assignment was the same the one held in our organization by Bob Tieken. I said it was. Then the conversation went like this:

Rick: Is there any doubt you can do the job?

Ira (after a few seconds of reflection): No.

Rick: Then why do you want it?

I didn't get that job. The next interview was to run a business within the Medical Systems Group: my first profit and loss responsibility at age 35. I was in that role for five years.

Take Away

Always look for personal growth and challenge.

Easy jobs are not rewarding.

Key Words

- *Challenge*
- *Competence*
- *Promotion*
- *Interviews*
- *Job interview*

Seeking Constant Personal Growth

1981

My predecessor as Division President of Medical Systems Financial Services business held an annual off-site strategic planning session. In my first year I invited Mike Vance (previously Director of Creativity for Walt Disney) to address my management team. I originally wanted him to "motivate" the organization to new heights. He told me no one can really motivate someone else. However, he would share some ideas with us.

He, like Rick Richardson (my mentor from my previous assignment at GE Locomotive), believed in being constantly challenged. Mike shared the following structured way of understanding where any of us are at any point in time regarding any field of endeavor:

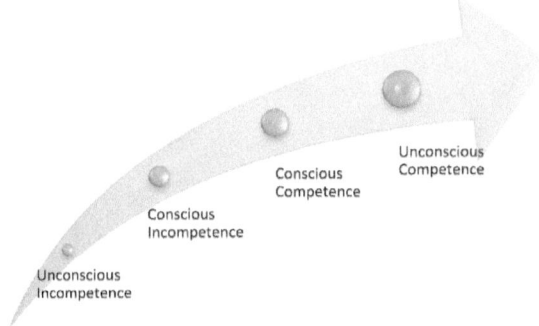

Unconscious Competence

Conscious Competence

Conscious Incompetence

Unconscious Incompetence

The trick is to know where one is within this model.

The goal is to find a new field of endeavor once one has reached the Unconscious Competence level to move to Unconscious

Incompetence. According to Mike, this is the way we increase our knowledge and stay challenged.

I have found this an excellent construct for my own development.

One of the benefits of Mike's lecture was that one of my staff members decided to leave GE and start his own business; a business that was ultimately very successful. Why a benefit? He was having a hard time accepting that after nine years of success the business needed to accelerate its growth.

Take Away

> *Committing oneself to constant growth keeps us energized, feeling good about ourselves, and willing to take reasonable risks to improve and grow.*

Key Words

- *Growth*
- *Personal growth*
- *Challenge*
- *Competence*

Career Growth

1976

I was approaching the end of my second year as CFO for the Transportation Group's Renewal Parts business; time for my annual appraisal.

Last year's appraisal, after my first year as a senior executive, was focused on areas for improvement within my assignment. In my second year I had settled in to the CFO role and was acting as the business' General Manager after the one I inherited left the job. I was feeling pretty good about my performance.

That's when Jack Kirker, the next layer CFO and my boss, called me in to his office. Jack told me he was about to start working on my annual appraisal. He wanted to know the criteria that I wanted him to use, the basis for the appraisal. I had two choices:

Choice I: use the responsibilities and requirements of my current CFO assignment. He came straight out and said if I chose this criterion, my appraisal would show all Excellent and Outstanding ratings (4s and 5s in a five-point system). This would also be the basis for my pay raise.

Choice II: compare my transferable skill level (skills needed in any senior executive position) to what will be required at the next higher organization layer. This will result in some individual area appraisal ratings of Marginal and Fully Satisfactory (2s and 3s). And, it could have an effect on my pay raise.

It was my choice.

I think it took one second for me to choose the second option. I was 30 years old and all I cared about was growing and learning.

Through this appraisal process Jack was able to give me an advanced look into the next higher layer at GE. We had a vehicle to discuss how expectations, communication, and politics would change and how I needed to grow in those areas.

Take Away

> *Use the system to address what needs to be addressed.*
>
> *Mentoring promotable subordinates is a critical part of leadership.*

Key Words

- *Career growth*
- *Mentoring*
- *Appraisal*

The Mentoring Obligation

1955

I didn't know my life would change when I entered Mrs. Hacker's fifth-grade class at PS 253 in Brooklyn, NY. I don't remember knowing at the time that I had been labeled as "behind in reading" and "slow learner," probably in first grade. Mrs. Hacker thought those labels were wrong. She had me re-tested. It turned out I was reading at the seventh-grade level and was not "slow."

Mrs. Hacker would periodically invite a number of her students to a gathering at her apartment. Her daughter, Iris, was also in fifth grade. We played Scrabble® and other games, had snacks. In summary, Mrs. Hacker took an interest in her students. She was probably my first mentor.

I was 10 years old in fifth grade. It's 57 years later, and Mrs. Hacker's mentoring is still with me. Imagine the impact we each can have over the next four decades if we successfully mentor three or so potential leaders each year for the rest of our working lives.

Take Away

> *Finding the rough diamond is a leadership responsibility.*
>
> *Mentoring can take place outside the office.*

Key Words

- *Mentoring*
- *Teaching*
- *Testing*

Impressions Matter

1977

There was no consistency in offices within the Locomotive Division. That led to wars about size, windows, etc. All non-productive activity when our job was to turn the business around. Also, with the exception of the executive suite, the walls were exposed brick, the windows better suited to a factory than an office, pipes were exposed as well. How could we feel good about ourselves when the clear message was that we didn't deserve a modern place in which to work?

It was for that reason that Rick Richardson (Division President) decided to completely renovate all the Locomotive office areas. That required setting standards and living by them.

At the final review of the standards, Rick made the only exception: the office of the Director – Materials (manufacturing) would be equal in size and amenities to that of the VP – Manufacturing.

His logic was simple. The Director-Materials job is responsible for (among other things) purchasing $6 billion (today's value) of material. The director is meeting with major vendors in that office. The office space itself MUST reinforce the level of responsibility associated with this job.

Take Away

Never let the rules get in the way of what's right.

Make sure to communicate the rationale for all decisions, especially those that break the rules.

Always consider how a decision will be viewed by the outside world.

Key Words

- *Rules*
- *Policy*
- *Breaking the rules*
- *Impressions*

Integrity Matters

1978

The Transportation Group reported to a Sector Executive who reported to GE's CEO (Reg Jones at the time). Rick Richardson was relatively new to running the Locomotive Division. The tenure of his boss, Carl Schlemmer, was only one year longer.

In August we were informed that Carl's new boss would be visiting the Erie plant for an initial business review in September. The new guy was previously in the Plastics Group: Jack Welch.

The Locomotive Division was by far the largest of all the organizations in GE's Erie, PA plant complex. Rick's presentation was massive, probably programmed to run 3+ hours. It covered everything from business environment to industry trends to competition down to individual programs and projects. But the story that emerged wasn't about numbers or programs. It was a lesson in leadership.

One small part of the Locomotive business was repairing the huge diesel engines that the railroads chose not to repair themselves. The business was called Unit Exchange (UX) because we sent out an exchange unit to the railroad as soon as they let us know they were sending the dead engine to our facility. I can't emphasize enough how insignificant this business was to the overall Locomotive results. But, in the financials, the UX numbers were down in the current year and Jack jumped all over Rick.

As the story goes (I wasn't in the meeting), Jack latched on to Rick like a junkyard dog.

Jack: Why are the UX numbers down?

Rick: The railroads can do these repairs themselves. When they have capacity available in their service shops, they don't send the engines to us.

Jack: What can you do to change that behavior?

Rick: Nothing. These are union shops. The railroads have to use that labor or pay for it anyway.

Jack: You need to do more.

Rick: These are our customers. We don't want to interfere with this and risk losing locomotive sales.

Jack: This is your business. You're telling me you can't get your customer to change!

Rick: Right. This is not the place to pick a fight.

Jack (very frustrated): Move on!

I don't know about you, but I would be dripping wet by the end of that exchange and figuring out how quickly I could get my resume up to date.

But, the story continues.

It turns out Jack's father was a railroad union worker. He fully understood the labor situation and fully understood the UX business model before coming to the Erie business review. This was his way to test Rick's mettle. Rick was the leader GE was betting on to turn around a business that employed 8,000 people. Jack wanted to know what kind of individual he had in this critical position.

Walking to lunch, Jack revealed his background to Rick. I heard the story from Rick. This is the way I remember it.

Take Away

Strong leadership is critical for success.

Maintain integrity no matter the perceived consequences.

Don't underestimate the level of knowledge or intelligence of the boss.

Key Words

- *Integrity*
- *Conviction*
- *Leadership*
- *Challenge*
- *Consequences*

The Wall Street Journal Test

1976

Rick Richardson's first assignment in the Transportation Group was Division President of a portfolio of businesses, one of which was building transit cars (subway cars for New York City, BART, etc.).

We had a large contract from the New York Transit Authority. Delivery would take place over several quarters. As with all GE businesses, we had quarterly reviews focused on financial results; comparing actual to forecast. These cars were put in the forecast based on expected production completion.

As planned, the first batch was ready for inspection and acceptance. The Transit Authority inspector reviewed the cars and found some items that did not meet his expectations. We missed our sales forecast for that quarter, but assured the Group's management that the fixed cars would generate sales in the next quarter.

The inspector reviewed the cars with the requested modifications and found additional problems. Again, we had to explain a miss against forecast.

This went on for an additional quarter. It was now a concern that the sales wouldn't occur in the current year. And, we didn't know what the inspector *would* accept. There was *extreme* pressure on management to get these sales. Frankly, the Group would miss all its targets if these sales didn't get booked. The Group's credibility with the Sector was at stake; not to mention bonuses.

As you can imagine, Rick and the staff were closely monitoring progress, with daily status reviews every morning.

At one of those meetings a manufacturing manager revealed that he had spoken with a friend who also supplied equipment to NYTA and had run into this inspector. The friend said the inspector was looking for a bribe before he would accept the equipment.

This started a debate in the room as to whether we should offer something to the inspector. What amount? How do you do this?

Rick let the conversation go on for a few minutes. He then asked a critical question:

"How would you feel if we do this and it appears on the front page of the *Wall Street Journal* tomorrow?"

That ended the bribe option.

Based on this information, Rick communicated the situation to Group and they to Sector. Contingency plans were put in place to protect the Sector's commitment to the Company, basically asking customers to take early delivery and pay for units currently scheduled for delivery next year.

Fast forward three weeks. Headlines in a Chicago (if I remember correctly) paper that this inspector had been arrested for taking bribes.

We had no trouble getting the equipment approved after that.

Take Away

This is the best ethics test I know of.

Think of all the horror stories that could have been avoided by asking this question (Enron, Arthur Andersen, the housing crisis, etc.).

Key Words

- *Ethics*
- *Decision making*
- *Wall Street Journal*
- *Bribes*

A Sale Isn't a Sale Until the Money Is Collected

1975

I had just been promoted to CFO of the Transportation Group's Renewal Parts business. It turns out I inherited a major receivables problem with the New York Transit Authority (NYTA); they were over one year past due. None of my predecessor's attempts at collection were remotely successful.

A few months later, Rick Richardson took over as president of the business unit Renewal Parts reported to. He called me and Ken McQuigan (Renewal Parts General Manager) in to his office to discuss this problem. Ken gave him all the details and excuses for not collecting – mostly having to do with fear of not getting any more orders from NYTA. Rick pointed out that an uncollected sale was not a sale at all.

I was tasked with putting together the plan to collect the outstanding receivable and to have NYTA pay timely for future purchases. John Collinear (my Manager – Sales Accounting) and I flew to New York to meet with NYTA's top purchasing manager. I was 29 years old, and John about the same.

I was born and raised in New York City. I was ready for the attitude we would get from the purchasing manager. He, however, was not ready for us. I'm sure he couldn't believe the lightweights GE had sent to resolve this. What he couldn't have known is that we had done our homework.

The short story goes like this:

After initial introductions, NYTA explained their fiscal problems. The purchasing manager threatened that they would use another supplier if we insisted on timely payment – they just didn't have the cash.

We told him we were prepared to shut them off, immediately, if we did not come to an agreement that day. (The fact was, this would shut down the NYC subway system in two or three months). He didn't believe GE would do that nor that I was authorized to make that decision. I gave him Rick's phone number.

He left to talk with his boss. I don't think they called Rick.

The deal: NYTA would pay off the existing receivable balance per a defined schedule (developed in this meeting) over the next 90 days. We would put them on 90-day terms which they would honor. There would be a "no tolerance" policy. Any missed payment would result in NYTA being shut off until they brought their account up to the agreement.

The agreement was confirmed in writing.

Except for some minor misses, they lived up to the agreement for my remaining time on that assignment.

Take Away

Do your homework before going in to negotiations.

Know where your walk-away is.

Have the backing of the ultimate decision-maker within your organization.

As the leader, ensure the above is in place and then let it play out; no second guessing.

Key Words

- *Collections*
- *Negotiations*
- *Receivables*
- *Decision making*
- *Second guessing*
- *Delegation*

Missed Cash Flow Commitment Trilogy – Story I

1977

One of the challenges for the GE Locomotive Division's new management team was to reverse years of negative cash flow. At GE we ran rolling three-month forecasts every month with an emphasis on results for the quarters and total year, including cash flow. My organization was responsible for, among other things, receivables collection, both domestic and international.

I was relatively new in my job, my second executive-layer assignment at GE. Rick Richardson, my mentor, was the new Division President. He got me the interview with Russ Rose, the Division's CFO. Russ and I had some rough going when I was in my previous assignment, but we put that behind us and he hired me. Another player in this story was Bob Tieken, CFO of the Transportation Group, and Russ's functional boss (Russ reported formally to Rick).

Gerry Sullivan was the Manager – Domestic Sales and Receivables. He had been on that assignment for five years or so, mostly under the previous Locomotive leadership. While he was knowledgeable about his job, he was in for a major change in expectations.

As I remember it, we were closing the March quarter. The reports came out around 11 AM and my group had missed $10 million in domestic collections. I understood this was unacceptable performance. We could never let this happen again.

I called Gerry in to my office and asked what happened. The specifics of the story aren't important (as if I could remember them). What I do remember is that the story was full of victimization; all the things we couldn't control. Based on everything I had learned from Rick and Jack Kirker (my previous boss and also a mentor of mine), this was not an acceptable attitude.

There was a large whiteboard in my office. I asked Gerry to write down all the steps he had just related to me, identifying which ones did not occur as planned – and then to write down what we could do to ensure they never happen again. It was lunch time and I wanted the task done by 1 PM. Over great protest, Gerry began his task.

I returned from lunch and Gerry was just finishing up. He had accomplished the mission by truly stretching his thinking about where we could change the process to increase our probability of success and what we could monitor to ensure critical steps were occurring as planned. (I should point out that collecting a domestic locomotive sale required that hard-copy paper be passed among the railroad, at least two banks, a financing company (and perhaps a guarantor), and all the associated attorneys – not a simple process.)

Gerry put the new system in place over the next 60 days with remarkable improvement in our domestic collections results (see Missed Cash Flow Commitment- Story III, below).

Take Away

> *Take accountability for everything that occurs within your area of responsibility.*
>
> *If you can't control each step, determine how to minimize the probability of a negative occurrence, or*
>
> *Set up an early warning system.*
>
> *Set high expectations.*
>
> *Delegate to experts: it's amazing to see them reach new heights.*

Key Words

- *Accountability*
- *Responsibility*
- *Out of the box*
- *Creativity*
- *Delegation*
- *Expectation*

Missed Cash Flow Commitment Trilogy – Story II

1977

You'll recall from the story *Missed Cash Flow Commitment – Story I,* my group missed the quarter's receivables collection by $10 million. And, that Gerry Sullivan, the manager responsible for that area, had developed a plan to ensure that we never missed our forecast for the same reason in the future.

An hour or so after Gerry finished his exercise, the phone rang. It was a furious Bob Tieken (Transportation Group CFO). He was also relatively new to his job. The Group's cash-flow forecast was being watched closely by GE Corporate. The entire leadership team's credibility was on the line. How the hell could I miss my forecast by $10 million, a forecast I made just 30 days ago! This miss had caused the Group to miss their commitment to Corporate. The decibel level was very high. Bob yelled at me for what was probably 30 seconds; it felt like an hour.

My response was: "You're right, I missed the forecast. I didn't know where the risks were. I didn't monitor the situation properly."

Bob was quiet. There was no use continuing to beat me up. I took responsibility.

Then I said: "Gerry has identified what went wrong and has a plan to ensure that it never happens again. We'd gladly show it to you."

Bob: "Just make sure it doesn't happen again."

From 11 AM that day, when we first saw the reports revealing the missed cash-flow forecast, until the end of that call with Bob Tieken, I thought my career at GE was over.

Take Away

As the leader, we are responsible for everything that happens in our unit, good and bad.

We leaders take all the heat for everything that goes bad. Performance issues with subordinates are handled separately.

We leaders give our subordinates credit for everything they do to help any situation.

Key Words

- *Accountability*
- *Responsibility*
- *Credibility*

Missed Cash Flow Commitment Trilogy – Story III

1977

This story wraps up the Missed Cash Flow Commitment trilogy.

Gerry Sullivan's plan was fine-tuned over the years. His organization's collection efforts became very proactive. Before his new process, domestic receivable days outstanding averaged around 180 days; GE collected its money half a year after shipping locomotives to the railroads. When I left the Locomotive Division in 1980, Gerry had gotten the number of days to zero. He was getting enough cash paid in advance of shipment to offset the small amount that was collected within 30 days after shipment. What a great job by Gerry and his team.

Take Away

Most people will reach higher expectations.

It is leadership's responsibility to raise expectations, reasonably, and consistently.

Key Words

- *Expectations*
- *Results*

Oops! I Said What I Meant

1975

My first executive layer position was CFO of the Renewal Parts Business at GE's Transportation Group. My mentor Jack Kirker (Division CFO) fought hard to get me in to that job. At 29 years old, many members of the Group's leadership thought I was wasn't ready for that level of responsibility.

The Division President whom Jack reported to was responsible for a diverse set of businesses and activities. He had two profit-and-loss centers and thee units that served the entire Transportation Group, one of which was Control Manufacturing (producing all the controls for every product line in the Group). Frank Schilling ran Control Manufacturing.

This year was particularly difficult for the Control Manufacturing unit. Frank was under a lot of pressure. They were having a hard time meeting production schedules and were spending significantly more than in their expense budget.

A month before Rick Richardson arrived as the new Division President, Frank wrote a letter in response to Group management's request for a plan to get his unit's performance on track. The letter focused almost exclusively on depreciation expense. His point was that GE's internal policy for depreciating the physical assets of the Control Manufacturing unit were not aligned with the tax depreciation the company was taking. And, that if the book policy were aligned with the tax rules, his expenses would be not be that far over budget.

What all this has to do with the Renewal Parts business is still a mystery to me. But, Jack gave me Frank's letter and asked me to respond.

My note back was pretty blunt. It basically said that the company's depreciation policy had not changed since the budget and was therefore not the issue. The issue was the management of Control Manufacturing, and I pointed out some of the more glaring performance variances from budget (i.e., direct labor utilization, cost of quality, headcount, etc.).

After a month on the job, Jack takes Rick through his first financial review for each of his businesses. When Rick asks about how Frank is responding to being behind in performance, Jack shows him Frank's letter and my response.

I get a call from Jack to come to his office (across the hall); no subject is mentioned. When I get there, Rick and Jack are standing next to each other.

To get the full effect of this scene I need to describe each of us. I'm 5'6" and weigh around 160 pounds. Jack is an athletic 5'11". Rick is a linebacker; over six feet weighing 260 or 270.

I walk into the outer office and Rick holds out my letter to Frank. "Did you write this!!!"

I take the letter in my hand. My hand is shaking. The letter has my signature on it. "Yes I did."

Rick smiles and says, "I like you. Good job."

That was my introduction to Rick Richardson, the best operating general manager I've ever known and, now, my mentor.

Take Away

> *Integrity is earned from doing the job well.*
>
> *The best leaders force their subordinates in to situations beyond their responsibilities and their comfort zones.*
>
> *Focusing on the business goal and taking the high road are almost always the best guidelines.*

Key Words

- *Integrity*
- *Stretch goals*
- *Responsibility*
- *Leadership*

Importance of the Personal Connection

1976

As Division President, Rick Richardson presented the division's results and future plans to the executives each quarter. A very extensive presentation was made annually to all employees. Rick encouraged all of his staff to do the same for their functional area of responsibility.

Jack Kirker (Division CFO) was reluctant to have this type of meeting since they were expensive and, as CFO, he thought finance should show strong financial restraint. After three years of prodding by Rick, Jack relented and had the first annual all-finance business review.

This was an unremarkable business review. Each of Jack's direct reports displayed what was going on in their unit. Jack discussed the division's results.

And then a remarkable turn of events took place. Jack started to talk about all the extra effort that had been expended by the assembled group. He started down a long list, with no notes, of special projects that supported the various businesses. With each project he mentioned the individuals who contributed. By the end of the presentation, Jack had thanked every person in the room, mentioning their names and linking them to the projects with which they were involved. With no notes!

The next day all the conversation was about how Jack knew every person in the Finance function.

Take Away

Quarterly and annual communication of business results are essential for building momentum toward company goals, and to build team playing.

Adding a personal touch to all communications resonates with the people in the organization regardless of the business message.

Key Words

- *Communication*
- *Annual meetings*
- *Quarterly meetings*
- *Personal touch*
- *Message*

First Advice

1968

I joined GE's Financial Management Program (FMP) three days after graduating from Pace College (now Pace University).

Shortly thereafter, all the FMPs in the Schenectady, NY location were invited to a dinner where a corporate executive would speak to the group. I can't remember who the executive was, but I do remember one part of his message.

This came after his prepared remarks. Someone from the audience, an FMP, asked what was the best way to get ahead at GE.

The executive's response was to latch on to a shooting star.

I remember thinking, wrongly, that we were being told that our performance didn't matter. All that mattered were connections.

As I think back on this first piece of advice in my corporate career, I realize that what was being suggested was to work with the best people. Associate with the best people. That will bring out the best in ourselves.

Take Away

Associating with the best people is the surest way to reach our goals.

Key Words

- *Growth*
- *Career*
- *Association*
- *Performance*

Educating the New Boss

1974

GE's Transportation Group was going through major organizational changes when I arrived in 1972. There were three profit and loss businesses (as I remember), Locomotive, Off-Highway Wheels, and Transit Cars. In early 1972 the manufacturing for Motors and Controls were each set up as separate P&L centers. Before then when motor manufacturing was under Locomotive, production was prioritized in favor of Locomotive. The reorganization was supposed to create prioritization based on the Group's best interest. It became clear that manufacturing P&Ls just don't make sense since they made their "profit" by, in effect, transferring inventory.

It took two years of multiple organizational reshuffling to get to the final, at the time, organization structure.

The Division that I became a part of had two stand-alone profit-and-loss centers (Off-Highway Wheels and Transit Components) and thee units that served the entire Transportation Group (Motor and Control manufacturing as cost centers and Renewal Parts as a P&L business). It was a very complicated leadership role for the Division President. He had to meet the financial objectives for his profit-and-loss centers while objectively supporting those business units and all the other P&L centers in the Group. Not only did he have to actually have each support organization behave equitably in the best interests of the Group, it had to be recognized as doing just that.

Over the first six months of 1974 we had four Division Presidents. Jack Kirker had been named CFO. Each new President needed to be brought up to speed. Since I was CFO for the Renewal Parts business, I participated in the education sessions.

It's not unusual for the new boss to be educated by his staff. In fact, we were excited to get the first one up to speed, thinking that this would solidify the management team and allow us to focus on the business.

His replacement was announced two months later. We went through the same exercise. We had to get used to a different personality and a different way of looking at the business. This one lasted one month.

The third President (all three were from within the Transportation Group) had seen the previous two fail. He knew he had only one month to prove himself. That pressure, added to his Type A personality, created a stress level I had never felt before. In addition, by now we were into GE's Strategic Planning cycle trying to discern the future for a bunch of businesses and manufacturing units when all we'd done for the year was educate new Presidents.

Thinking back, the Group President must have started the search for a new Division President when he appointed Division President Number 3. Rick Richardson showed up two months later.

I remember this time as dark and exhausting. Maybe it was because my office was across the hall from Jack's, but it seems he and I were always working late into the night (10 PM to mid-night). The education process took much of the day and then we had to get the regular work done (close the books, report results, forecast presentations, strategic reviews, etc.).

Jack's favorite saying during this time was: "The plumbers are home drinking beer." He never let on to how frustrated he must have been. He just kept on keeping on. Getting his work done. Counseling others to stay focused.

Rick was his reward. Rick became Jack's mentor as well. Jack eventually became Division President (Rick's job). Years later, he left GE to run a business unit for AT&T. Sold that unit to Siemens. Financially secure, Jack and his wife retired to California.

Take Away

Educating the new boss is part of our job.

Perseverance has its rewards.

Key Words

- *New boss*
- *Perseverance*

Leadership Philosophy 101

1966

I spent two years at SUNY-Albany between graduating from Staten Island Community College and attending Pace College (graduated 1968). My wife says my only reason for being at SUNY-Albany was to meet her. Forty-six years later she's still the light of my life.

We met in Dr. Hoagland's Organization Development class. The only other thing I remember about this class was a two-day exercise that set my philosophy on leadership.

Day One: Dr. Hoagland met us at the door to his classroom. Every so often he appointed one of the students as the Manager; all the others were workers. He pointed out to each of us a model (a chicken made from Tinker Toy pieces) on one of the desks. We were divided up in to four work groups, each with a Manager and a Tinker Toy box, and told to build a replica of the model chicken; as many as possible and as quickly as possible. Once we were all inside, he stormed around the room firing Managers when the group didn't meet his expectations of speed or quality. He continued with this for 20 minutes or so. We were then dismissed for the day; not one chicken completed.

Day Two: Dr. Hoagland met us at the door to his classroom. Every so often he appointed one of the students as the Manager; all the others were workers. He pointed out to each of us a model (Tinker Toy chicken) on one of the desks. We were divided up in to four work groups, each with a Manager and a Tinker Toy box, and told to build a replica of the model; as many as possible and as quickly as possible.

But this time he made no adjustments. In fact he left the area. When he returned, about 20 minutes later, each group had made at least one chicken. Our group's first chicken matched the model exactly (each piece's color) and we were working on exchanging pieces with another group to complete our second chicken.

Take Away

Set the expectation and get out of the way.

Micro-management is never the answer.

Key Words

- *Leadership*
- *Delegation*
- *Micro management*

Corporate Bigamy

1976

Dr. Mortimer R. Feinberg, PhD isn't a household name nor does the name come trippingly off the tongue, nor did his resume say much about him. Yet it was my responsibility to host and introduce him as the last instructor to my Managers Development Course at GE's Crotonville campus.

GE has long been known for its cradle-to-grave education philosophy. When it comes to leadership, there were three, month-long courses that were rites of passage: Managers Development Course (MDC: for managers about to lead a function [think VP-Marketing]); Business Managers Course (BMC: before becoming a P&L general manager [division President]); and Executives Development Course (EDC: before having responsibility for multiple P&L centers).

It was an honor to be nominated for one of these courses and a great experience to go through them. They were one full month at Crotonville, GE's internal college campus, completely removed from one's job.

The penultimate evening, the last Thursday of the month, was our first night in 25 that we didn't have case studies to go through on top of other reading or simulation exercise decisions. It included a gourmet meal, a lot of wine, and after dinner reminiscing and cocktails. We were a tough audience for whoever was our last instructor on Friday morning. For our class it was Mortimer Feinberg.

Dr. Feinberg captured us almost immediately with his energy, his knowledge, and his messages. There were many, but none as important, to me, as corporate bigamy.

His premise was that we, as future leaders at GE, would have to devote more time to the Company. The Company would become, in effect, our second wife (or mistress). He went on to explain how this would affect our spouses and children. NOTE: we were still in a time when business leadership was mostly male and wives, no matter how well educated, chose to be stay-at-home moms.

His insights were, frankly, revealing and touching. He spoke about the relationship with his children and the tensions caused by his responsibilities as Department Chairman at City College of New York.

He gave us one piece of advice as it relates to business travel that I'd like to pass on to you. Think about the standard scenario:

You return home after being on the road for a week or two. Constantly "on" with customers and employees, listening non-stop to problems. Eating out three meals a day. You come home and what does your wife want?... to go out to dinner. To get out of the house. To share with you what has been going on. To unload about the kids, her Mom, your Mom, house chores, house maintenance. This is the last thing you want to do. Dr. Feinberg's advice: GO TO DINNER. LISTEN. INTERACT.

But it doesn't end there. Dr. Feinberg suggested that we make love with our wives that first night home. It's pretty obvious isn't it? A reconnection. A reaffirmation of the relationship.

Since 1982 our lives seem to have become more hectic, more separate, more *individual*. Today, both spouses are at work all day, and/or traveling on business. Dr. Feinberg's advice is all that more relevant today than ever.

Take Away

Understand the strain that success puts on one's spouse and family.

Two tips for retaining your spousal relationship and being successful at the same time.

Key Words

- *Success*
- *Spouse*
- *Family*
- *Relationship*

Only Private Negotiations Work

1976

Here's the exercise:

Three teams, with roughly 12 people per team, are asked to design a trophy to be given, at a later time, to the group that wins the business simulation game. The teams are given an hour to come up with the design. Then, the captains of each team will meet to determine which trophy will be used.

This is a true story from GE's Managers Development Course.

My team had no trouble designing the physical trophy or developing the words to be engraved on it. We spent some time on the "selling points" for our captain's meeting. At the end of the hour we were invited to "the Pit," a round classroom where the teaching area was "sunk" in the middle and the students' desks rose up, each successive row higher than the one in front of it.

Each team's Captain was in the lowest row, closest to the teaching area, while the rest of each team sat in the rows behind the Captain, in the same section. The Captain was alone in the negotiation (team members could not speak). Each entire team was sitting directly behind their captain, watching and listening.

After an hour of discussion, no decision. The Captains got close once, but that ended quickly. Our session leader (instructor) was about to call a stalemate, but the Captain's begged for more time. They were given another 15 minutes. At the end, no agreement. The exercise ended without meeting the stated objective.

The instructor informed us that no group had ever reached agreement!

The takeaway for me was the realization that negotiations MUST be done in private if they are to have a chance of being successful. The cold fact is that the negotiator (Captain) must be able to modify his or her stance in order to reach agreement – something that is almost impossible to do when constituencies are applying pressure for their original point of view (even silently, by just being there).

Take Away

Final negotiations require that the decision-makers meet to craft a compromise.

Negotiations will be more effective if the participants are limited to only the decision-makers and their closest advisors.

Key Words

- *Negotiation*
- *Decision*
- *Decision-making*
- *Compromise*

A Different Marketing Plan

1982

FAIR WARNING: THIS STORY MY AFFEND SOME PEOPLE
DUE TO SOME SUGGESTIVE CONTENT

In the early 1980s the Japanese car manufacturers had gained a foothold in the U.S. market with higher gas mileage and better fit and finish than the American auto makers. GE wanted those of us in the Business Managers Course to understand how Company Japan was succeeding.

In one exercise we were divided in to small teams (say eight people) with the goal of developing the marketing campaign for Honda motorcycles, just entering the United States market. We had one hour. We would be presenting our ideas to the full group when we returned to the classroom. The Business Managers Course was in to its second week at this time, so we knew each other fairly well at this point.

Our group quickly identified the benefits, features, and competitive situation. After 30 minutes or so we stepped back and decided our story was boring and would look the same as all the others about to be presented. Then someone had a break-through thought: The Honda bikes were smaller than Harleys, easier to handle, you can get your feet on the ground when the bike is stopped – perfect for women. How could we appeal to women? The answer: convert the seat so that the vibration from the bike's engine could be felt in the driver's crotch. In essence, turn the bike into a vibrator. This led to our slogan: "Come on a Honda." We quickly put our story together on chart paper and returned to the classroom; our leader prepared to make his presentation.

What a surprise when we entered the classroom to find three people from Corporate in the room to hear the presentations; two men and one woman! As it turned out, they were sitting were I could easily see their faces.

Frankly, I wasn't sure what our leader was going to do. He just went forward as we had planned. He explained our view of the untapped, woman's market. Pointed out how a smaller bike would be more comfortable for that demographic. And then hit them with the slogan: "Come on a Honda." The audience erupted in laughter. I looked over at our guests. All were smiling. I had the sense that our female executive was working hard at not laughing out loud.

Take Away

Having fun with and applying humor to a task can bring out unexpected, creative results.

Tell the story the way you envision it – let the audience deal with the consequences.

Key Words

- *Truth to power*
- *Creativity*
- *Fun*
- *Humor*
- *Brainstorming*

GE Business Simulations

1982

One common instruction tool at both the Managers Development Course and the Business Managers Course was a business simulation competition that ran for three weeks.

Each team was a different business entity competing against the other teams. The opening scenarios were different; each team viewing the market differently, but having the same market information. As with all simulations, each team set its strategy, made operating decisions, executed its plans, and reacted to unexpected market changes and random events.

My MDC experience is a blur. We didn't win; may have come in last. But, at the end of BMC (didn't win this one either), what GE was trying to teach us became very clear to me.

Those teams that did the worst viewed each hurdle that was thrown at them by the simulation as a challenge to their basic strategic assumptions. An unexpected seasonal drop or spike in demand resulted is a knee-jerk reaction to production. Or, the impact of an unfavorable news article was seen as requiring a change is strategy.

The winners stuck with their strategy and consistently executed against that strategy. They viewed these same challenges as distractions that had to be handled, but were able to take a broader view of the situation.

Take Away

Strategy sets the framework for future decision-making.

A steady hand regarding changes from strategy leads to smaller, incremental adjustments.

Incremental change is easier for an organization to accept and easier to reverse if it proves to be ill advised.

Yin/Yang decision-making never proves to be successful.

Key Words

- *Decision-making*
- *Strategy*
- *Strategic planning*
- *Change*
- *Change management*

Work the System

1985

This story is a little involved, but stick with it; I think it might start some creative juices flowing.

GE Capital's Vendor Financing business bought Bank of America's computer leasing business (Decimus Corporation) in early 1985 (maybe late 1984). I reported in as GE Computer Leasing's first President in August 1985, after five years at the helm of GE's Medical Systems Financial Services Division.

At the time, all "true leases" had one thing in common, the leasing company took some level of risk that the equipment would have value at the end of the lease; this is called "residual value."

All the GE Capital leasing Divisions established the residual values on the products they leased by applying their years of experience with those products or as established by third parties, either through a special study commissioned by the GE Capital Division or as published in reliable industry journals. I believe all the non-computer leases had terms under which the cost of the equipment was recovered by the contracted length of the lease. That is, a $1.0 million machine on lease had contracted payments that would exceed the $1.0 million of initial cost. Therefore, the only risks were (1) non-payment by the lessee, or (2) the rate of return if the residual value was not realized. The residual values for non-computer equipment generally remained stable and therefore, could be predicted well enough for five years. As a result, residual studies were commissioned every five years or so, and those estimates were used for deal pricing (to get targeted ROI) until the next study was completed.

Mainframe computers were totally different.

First, due to their high-technology nature, customers wanted the lease term (length) to be only three years or less. That meant that the lease revenues would not cover the initial purchase cost during the initial lease term.

Second, the residual values could change significantly when new models were introduced by the manufacturers, especially if there was no upgrade path from the current equipment to the new series. Two industry groups published estimated residual values every three and four months respectively.

Third, non-residual risk needed to be limited since the residual risk was so great. Therefore, we invested only in IBM equipment, and our customers were the Fortune 50.

Fourth, any forecasted drop in estimated residual value required that we develop a customized upgrade plan (technology and financing) for any customers who might want to return (what would be) obsolete equipment at the end of the lease.

In a nutshell, computer leasing moves at a speed that is significantly faster than most equipment leasing activity.

OUR CHALLENGE: how do we get deals processed through the GE Capital system when almost nothing in the computer leasing model matches everything else going through GE Capital?

INITIAL FAILURE: I was able to learn about Decimus's business model before the remnants of Decimus's leadership left in frustration after the acquisition. When we tried to put through a deal, it got rejected because, using the GE Capital formulas, we couldn't hit the ROI targets. Frustration mounted. The previous Decimus leadership was pre-disposed against GE Capital as a competitor: They all left when they saw that authority was moving from our Division to Corporate.

UNDERSTANDING THE GAME: Like so many breakthroughs, this one looks easy in retrospect, but I can assure you I, too, was blinded by frustration at the time. I called some trusted associates at the next layer up to get their thoughts on our predicament. After all, GE Capital is a large organization: perhaps some other unit had figured out how to book business given our situation. The solution came from our Group CFO. He said: "You know there's an exception process." Rather than submitting a deal through the computerized review system (where it got rejected), we could do a formal write-up asking for special permission to do the deal. Called "a story deal," we would have to explain the specific circumstances of each transaction (why the equipment was worthy of investment, credit write-up of the customer, justification of the residual value, etc.). No generalizations. No referring back to previously approved deals. Each deal stands on its own.

REALIGNING THE TEAM: If all our deals were going to be exceptions, three things needed to change in our business:

1. Everyone needed to understand and sign on to the level of work that was going to be required if we were going to be successful. This was shared within every offer letter to potential vice-presidents as I was replacing the previous Decimus executives.

2. We needed someone to write up the deals. This position would synergize the entire transaction in to a cogent story; it was much more than a Credit Analyst, but that was the title and job description already blessed and available within GE Capital. So we used it with the agreement of my boss, his boss, and Human Resources. We had to bust through the pay scale to get the right individual.

    One other point, my executive team had to be behind every deal we sent up for approval. Once the deal was understood, and before the formal write-up, we would meet, discuss, get more info if needed, and decide as a team. The Credit Analyst's signature on the write-up was a proxy for all of us.

3. Finally, there was a need to act faster in the market than we could internally. This meant we would take deals off the street before having approval, or going through the full evaluation. If a deal was not approved or we chose not to advance it, how would we honor our commitment to the customer? Our solution: outplace the deal with another leasing company or bring in an equity backer for the deal. This was yet another executive position on my staff. Once again we searched for approved position guides, found one, got permission to hire, and found the right person.

WHAT WAS THE RESULT? My team worked extremely hard to make our business successful. It was one of a few situations in my career where we were firing on all eight cylinders.

In each of the two years I was associated with the business, we tripled our new business budget and the business received GE Capital's *Best Business* award each year.

Take Away

Obstacles can be opportunities when looked at the right way.

Seeking advice and insights from others can help reduce obstacles (walls to hurdles, hurdles to speed bumps, speed bumps to smooth riding).

Key Words

- *Out of the box*
- *Creativity*
- *Obstacles*
- *Initiative*
- *Team playing*

When a Success Formula Backfires – Part I

1986

It is helpful to have read *Work the System* before reading this and the next story.

In our second year at GE Computer Leasing, we were brought in to a very different type of deal than our typical customer lease. This was a manufacturer looking to borrow funds to complete its latest software development and launch that product. We were asked to consider the deal because we were part of GE Capital. This deal, by itself, represented 25 percent of our annual, new business budget.

We applied the same exception process discussed in the *Work the System* story. The company was the largest supplier to an industry segment. The deal was structured with multiple guarantees. Basically, if the company defaulted, we would own them and all their intellectual property. We delivered the write-up to Corporate after having many discussions, sharing drafts of the write-up, and having oral approval.

While this was going on, our Group executive was promoted within GE Capital and a new one appointed. Our new Group Executive and I had a long, positive history dating to my Medical System days. Chuck was, in my estimation, an excellent businessman, leader, and a straight shooter.

After a relatively short review period, our deal was rejected. The team had put in months of effort into this transaction; going between the customer and Corporate to get a win-win structure. All the feedback had been positive.

The news of the rejection knocked the wind out of the entire organization, not just the executive staff. How could it go bad after all the effort to get internal agreement in advance? And all we got was a rejection, no explanation. It took weeks to build morale back so we were a fighting team again.

WHAT REALLY HAPPENED

At GE Capital's annual kick-off retreat six months later I sought out Chuck. He brought me in to GE Capital. I felt comfortable asking why we got rejected on this deal. He told me that it was his personal policy to reject the first deal from any group when he was the new boss. He felt that sent a message to raise the bar. I shared with him that this time it had the exact opposite reaction.

WHAT HAPPENED TO THE DEAL?

Remember our outplacement executive? She sold the deal to another company. We made a nice broker fee.

Take Away

We all need to periodically challenge our success formulas.

Sometimes even the best work, with the best intentions, fails.

We learn a lot from failure; how to do things differently, and about ourselves.

Key Words

- *Failure*
- *Success formula*
- *Rejection*
- *Recovery*
- *Decision-making*

When a Success Formula Backfires – Part II

1987

At GE Capital's annual kick-off meeting, I was taken aside by my boss for a private discussion. We had just finished our first year in the newly acquired GE Computer Leasing business. We had completely replaced the executive team, developed the methodology to get deals processed, decided on which technology to bet on, and aggressively entered the market. The result: we tripled our new business budget.

Our second year's budget was the same as in the previous year (1/3 of previous year's actual). That was due to concerns with accumulated residual risk.

My boss shared with me that his new business budget for the current year was in jeopardy. He had two businesses and the other one was in trouble. Therefore, my business needed to overachieve to a number that was almost *seven times* our official budget.

Remember, we had to get every deal approved through a tortuous exception process. Our ability to find, close, write up, and defend each deal was probably at capacity at the last year's level. Maybe, with some good luck, we could do triple again (and we did), but seven times was out of the question. In fact, I believed that merely requesting this level of volume from my staff would reduce our effectiveness, since the definition of success would be seen as impossible.

THE OUTCOME

I was told to bring this challenge to my organization. I did. It had the effect of deflating rather than invigorating the group. It also had the effect of putting my boss and me at odds with each other. He was reporting upwards that he would make his budget. It eventually became obvious he would miss his budget. By then, our relationship could not be salvaged.

I left. A new president was appointed. The team broke up. New leadership appears to have gone for volume; profits suffered. Computer leasing was just too different. Ultimately, GE Capital exited the business.

Take Away

Stretch targets need to be seen as reasonable by those that must reach them.

Organizations need to understand the drivers of failure.

Key Words

- *Stretch targets*
- *Failure*

When Good Enough Works

1999

In the *Big Stories* section of this book there is a story about Trex Medical, *Reorganizing Marketing and Sales at Trex Medical*. That story was about the business decisions we had to make. This one is about the personnel.

Let's start with the obvious. There are four fully staffed divisions. At the end, we will have one unified company. That means jobs will be eliminated and people will be laid off.

We also know that these divisions, before they were acquired by Trex Medical, were stand-alone businesses: minnows in a sea of whales (GE, Siemens, Philips, Toshiba). They fought fiercely against each other. Nothing much changed when they became part of Trex Medical, they continued to dislike each other and fight each other in the marketplace.

The leadership at each of the divisions were very knowledgeable about their individual business. But, they were, generally, not sophisticated leaders. As Rick Richardson (GE division President and my mentor) would say: "They had 25 years experience, one year's experience 25 times".

I arrived in March 1999 knowing the challenge was consolidation. The first few months were spent learning the individual businesses and getting the organizations to develop a unified vision for Trex's future. With that done, it was necessary to establish the organization (structure and people) that would handle the very difficult next phase: consolidating the distribution channels and product lines.

This was going to be a personal exercise, no delegation involved. Here are the steps I took.

First, I identified all the assignments we would need to fill; drawing blank boxes on the organization chart. This was for every position in Marketing and Sales, not just my direct reports. Each had five to ten critical responsibilities identified. Human Resources helped me in filling out position descriptions so that I had a complete document to talk from.

One of the outcomes of this exercise was identification of assignments that didn't exist in any of the divisions. That meant fewer layoffs with the benefit of retaining historical knowledge.

Second, I needed to decide on my direct reports; they would then develop their own organization chart and recommend with whom to populate it. This was extremely difficult. Remember, we had more than one person doing each job and most of them were not fully qualified to have that same assignment for a company four times larger than their current division.

Third, once the staff was in place, they would need to fill in each open assignment.

Fourth, all the people in the new organization would have to rationalize the product lines and distribution channels in time for us to have a cogent story at the industry gathering, Radiology Society of North America (RSNA), just six months later, at the end of November.

THE PERSONNEL DECISION

Normally I would want to get the best possible person, within or outside the company. Outside became out of the question. We didn't have the time to even find five of six senior people, much less have them get up to speed and make the decisions in time for RSNA. The only solution was to choose from the existing management ranks.

I did the best I could from what I had learned about each person in the business reviews and subsequent conversations. I'll never know if I could have made better decisions. I do know it was good enough.

With a tremendous amount of hard work on the critical business issues and rebuilding relationships, the team accomplished the critical goals and got us ready for RSNA. We had a credible story. Order rates for December and January were up. We were in position to execute our plan.

However, at the end of January 2000, our parent Company decided to put Trex Medical up for sale. It was part of an effort for Thermo-Electron to get back to its core business, making it easier for

Wall Street analysts to understand the business and in turn improve its shareholder value. We were one of 60 division sold that year. Thermo's stock price increased. It was a good strategy for them.

Take Away

Sometimes we need to work with what we have.

Setting clear short-term goals helps focus oneself and the team.

Always start with the organization boxes when laying out an organization structure. Fill in the people afterward, never reverse the process.

Key Words

- *Short term goals*
- *Organization structure*
- *Personnel*

Share the Problem

1999

One of the major, short-term challenges at Trex Medical was to rationalize four overlapping and competing distribution channels into a single trained, competent, and aggressive distributor network.

There was one distributor that was much larger than all the rest. Actually, probably close to the size of all the others combined. Physicians Sales & Service (PSS) lobbied strongly that their size commanded that they get special treatment in Trex's distribution strategy. They seemed to have a good story and a lot of leverage.

Meanwhile, we had other distributors who, while smaller, were equally competent and more effective in their territory than PSS.

Working with my newly appointed VP-Sales, John Garrett, we started with data: orders and sales volumes over the last few years, sliced and diced by modality and customer type. We added anecdotal information from long-term marketing and salespeople. All of this led to no conclusion – nothing popped out as an obvious solution.

During this time all the distributor owners were on the phone with me making their cases. We talked a lot. I got to know them a bit and something about their philosophies of doing business. I gained respect for how they viewed their business, their loyalty to their customers and employees.

What did emerge was that there were five distributors (other than PSS) who I believed had exceptional insights in to their business and ours. I invited them to a brainstorming session.

That first session was mostly John and me sharing our problem with them. We showed them all our analysis. We asked what would they do if they were in our shoes. They agreed to take on the assignment of coming back with a unified recommendation.

In the second session the distributors presented their recommendation. It was basically "Kill PSS." We did a lot of probing.

There was some good underlying thought, but our sensitivity to PSS was clearly much greater than theirs. John and I went away disappointed with the result.

We continued to work the problem. Our industry meeting, RSNA, was rapidly approaching. We needed to let our distributors know one way or another how they related to Trex Medical. Frankly, PSS's size story was starting to win us over. Then the phone rang.

It was the "chair" of our distributor committee. The group had continued to talk after the second meeting. They had an approach they wanted to share.

The third meeting was all listening from our part. The committee suggested that we needed to define "the market" not as the United States, but break it down in to individual, regional markets. That would convince us that their original recommendation was the way to go.

The regional markets idea made sense to us, but it wouldn't generate the result expected by the committee.

We reran our original orders and sales analysis based on a logical regional dissection of the Country. To our surprise, in almost every region there was a clear winner. PSS's candidate in each region was the sum of their districts in that region; so they never got a benefit for national coverage. We gave each defined territory to the best performing distributor in that territory.

We explained our approach and decisions to each of the affected distributors. PSS was not happy, but they went forward with us, having won a fair number of the regions based on merit. As it turns out, the distributor committee members did very well. After all, we asked for their help based on our view of the quality of their leadership.

Take Away

> *Too many leaders feel it's their job to make all the decisions. Sharing that responsibility not only unburdens the leader, it also results in more alternatives, many better than the leader's initial thought.*

Key Words

- *Problem resolution*
- *Delegation*
- *Committees*

The Importance of Net Worth

2000

Entrepreneurial consultants concern themselves with satisfying customers and making enough profit to support their family. Those of us in larger companies concern ourselves with doing our job well, status or station within the organization, and compensation. All of these are valid and important. But missing is the most important of all: Net Worth.

At the end of the day, our financial independence is not based on what we earned, but on what we kept.

A long while ago an associate of mine said: "I'm just a transfer station. I bring it in and my wife sends it out." Funny at the time.

Now I understand how true and pervasive that comment is; and how negatively it impacts some very smart, hard-working families.

The forced sale of Trex Medical had an unsettling but positive impact on me and my family. We were in our newly built house in New Fairfield, CT for just six months when I came home with the news that Trex would be sold. I calmed myself down by telling my wife, Kathy, that I'd get my resume together and start calling my executive search contacts within the next few days. I figured that would reduce her anxiety as well. I was shocked when she came back saying that she was tired of giving her house away every five years (we were in our tenth home at that point). She wanted to know if we could find our "retirement" home and settle in. I called our financial planner, David Deming, to get his thoughts. He said we should be fine. That's what brought us to Pinehurst.

We had been working with David since 1994 with a plan to retire in 2010. As a result of his good advice and a few promotions, we were at financial independence in 2000. Financial independence comes from net worth.

My consulting practice has allowed us to withstand the impact of two recessions on our investments. We're fortunate once again.

My point is, business leaders need to understand that attention to their net worth is as important as compensation, the size of the office, the title on the door. I like to see my clients have a "life plan" that leads to financial independence.

Take Away

Financial independence should be a goal of every executive and business owner.

Key Words

- *Financial independence*
- *Personal decision-making*

CLIENT STORIES

Here are a few true stories about how my clients handled a situation. Each has specific take away lessons for The High Yield Consultant to deliver to their prospects or clients.

In this section, all the names (people and companies) have been camouflaged. Also, I've taken some creative license with the stories to get to the point more quickly or make the story more interesting.

Customer Concentration

Let me share a real-life story with you.

Kyle is the second generation Owner/CEO of his Company. The Company's survival was in jeopardy when their largest customer (of only eight customers) was acquired by a company with a long-standing relationship with Kyle's primary competitor. The revenue loss put the Company at negative cash flow even after Kyle took action to reduce costs. Kyle knew his business and had excellent leadership instincts. However, he believed he was, in addition to CEO, the CSO (Chief Solutions Officer). This isolated him in his decision-making. Kyle hated conflict and avoided it at almost all cost. He also found public speaking to be very difficult.

In Kyle's case, the lost customer caught him by surprise, but he was determined not to let that happen again. He knew the answer was to have many more customers so as not to be so dependent on any one customer. The concern: could his organization handle the additional workload and still maintain its high level of customer service and product quality?

Kyle really had two problems: (1) getting the organization prepared for the larger customer base, and (2) improving his leadership skills in the area of conflict resolution and communication.

With some coaching, Kyle shared his vision of a larger customer base and his fears with the organization. Through a series of seminars and workshops, the management team learned about alternative organizational structures. They settled on one and went about the restructuring, becoming more market driven without losing their customer focus or manufacturing quality.

Their customer base increased significantly over the next few years.

Then the Great Recession of 2008 hit. Kyle's business was affected as were all in his industry.

This time he framed the situation for his management team; provided guidelines for keeping the business going. Then he let the management team come up with their solutions to meet his guidelines. They made the changes necessary to weather the storm and increased market share during the recession. The business has retained their higher market share as the their industry is recovering.

The CFO tells me Kyle has become more confident as a leader. By sharing the business' problems with the organization, he finds communicating is easier.

Oh, and Kyle has retired from his Chief Solutions Officer position.

Take Away

Market shares improve in down cycles more than in up cycles.

The organization has insights that the leadership team does not have.

Leaders can improve their business by "leading" rather than being the Chief Solutions Officer.

Key Words

- *Delegation*
- *Market share*

Cash Flow

Opportunities were raining down on Craig's Company and they were unable to take advantage of any of them. Craig hired a COO to help run the existing business units so that Craig could pursue new areas of growth for the Company.

A few months later, Craig was in contact with a previous customer-turned-consultant (me). He knew something was wrong: revenues were up but profits were down. He couldn't get a reasonable explanation from his controller.

I worked with the controller to understand the business processes by reviewing the books. Two revelations emerged:

1. The new COO had instituted a Company-wide reward system based on current month's financial results. In a month when the business showed a profit, some of it was passed on to the management and employees. But, when there was a loss, the Company ate it. Since the Company was in three businesses, none of which had steady revenue, the employees were doing very well, so well that the Company was reporting less profit; year over year.

2. Each of the three business unit's revenue streams was cyclical. That made it very difficult to predict cash flow. In fact, the controller didn't understand the concept of a cash cycle. Using the controller's knowledge of the business, I developed the Company's cash cycle. Then the Company's cash flow was projected out for three months based on the new model. The result: the Company would run out of cash in 10 weeks or so. A surprise to everyone.

Craig called his team together and asked me to share what we had learned. The group identified the only cash source available in the near term: advance payments for a scheduled seminar the Company put on every year. Everyone hit the phones to get the advance payment from likely attendees. It worked. Crisis avoided.

The more permanent solution involved improving their cash cycle process. One area was billing and collections. The Company would call customers once their invoices were 15 days past due. Craig implemented my recommendation to call accounts on the due date if payment was not received.

I also recommended that the Company invoice 30 – 60 days before the contractual due date; thereby giving even the largest customers time to have the paperwork flow through their accounts payable process. Craig also changed this process.

As a result of understanding their cash flow reality – and that Craig was not willing to invest more capital into the business – Craig focused the Company's efforts on one of the three businesses; which ultimately became the whole business.

Craig sold the Company a few years later at a substantial profit.

Take Away

Leaders must understand their financials, especially cash flow.

Blindly pursuing growth and/or expansion can be devastating.

Key Words

- *Financial statement*
- *Cash flow*
- *Strategy*
- *Cash cycle*
- *Billing*
- *Collections*

Time to Move On

I had been working with this Company (PWI) at the corporate layer and with two of the division Presidents. It was at dinner with the CEO and his wife that the idea of his retirement came up. Will, the CEO, was past "normal" retirement age, but loved his Company. He reported to a board of family members, some of whom were new to the board as older members relinquished their seats. The conversation was actually very light and humorous. But I tucked it away for a future, private discussion with Will.

A few months later Will and I were finishing up a planned meeting when he brought up some feelings he was having about his board. As I remember it, the new board members were gently challenging some of Will's decisions. I must stress that Will did not feel threatened. But, this was very different from the normal rubber stamp he was used to. I used this as an opportunity to ask about Will's retirement plans.

This really touched a nerve. By the end of his monologue, I felt I had used up almost all my relationship capital with him in the one question. I backed off. The meeting ended.

Will brought up the friction with his board in our following meeting. And then again during the next. As his advisor, I had to raise "retirement" again, no matter the consequences. This time I got a very different monologue. He was concerned about what he would do if not coming to work each day. Will had numerous outside interests. In fact, he was the most Renaissance-like person I'd ever known. So, that wasn't the real issue. We kept talking. Will finally asked: "What would you do?"

That was my opportunity to get to the whiteboard and start drawing the process Will would need to go through to get the business ready for a new leader. We talked about everything from the impact on specific individuals to the qualifications for his replacement to getting the board ready for a non-family CEO.

Will and his corporate leadership team executed the plan over the next year or so. Today there is a new President/CEO in place who has the respect of the PWI's leaders and operating managers.

Take Away

> *There's a time and place to handle the truly difficult issues. Wait for the disease to emerge before attempting a remedy.*

Key Words

- *Life plan*
- *Disease*
- *Symptom*
- *Succession planning*

SAYINGS AND ONE-LINERS

Sometimes the best education comes from a simple statement that resonates with the student. I've been adding phrases to this section as they pop up in my head. They will either immediately make sense to you or not. Use the ones you're comfortable with; ignore the others.

- No one is hired to maintain the status quo or make things worse.
- The job of leadership is to identify the need for and implement change.
- People don't mind change, they mind *being* changed.[2]
- Share the problem, not the solution.
- Don't compound change.
- In 2011, 79 percent of senior executives believe complexity of doing business will increase over the next five years.[3]
- 92 percent of change management efforts fail.[4]
- 86 percent of management consulting assignments fail[5]
- Our job is to get the boss promoted.
- The plumbers are home drinking beer.
- Managers do things right. Leaders do the right thing.[6]

---

[2] Peter Bregman
[3] Global CEO Survey, IBM, June 2010
[4] 2001 IMC National Meeting, presentation by Peter Bregman
[5] 2001 IMC National Meeting, presenter unknown
[6] Peter Drucker

---

[i] *Playing to Win,* Larry Wilson and Hersch Wilson
[ii] Maxiservice® is a registered trademark of GE Medical Systems

www.ingramcontent.com/pod-product-compliance
Lightning Source LLC
Chambersburg PA
CBHW022000170526
45157CB00003B/1082